AGAINST THE TIDE

AGAINST THE TIDE

Love in a Time of Petty Dreams
and Persisting Enmities

Miroslav Volf

WILLIAM B. EERDMANS PUBLISHING COMPANY

GRAND RAPIDS, MICHIGAN / CAMBRIDGE, U.K.

Published 2010 by

Wm. B. Eerdmans Publishing Co.

2140 Oak Industrial Drive N.E., Grand Rapids, Michigan 49505 /

P.O. Box 163, Cambridge CB3 9PU U.K.

www.eerdmans.com

Printed in the United States of America

15 14 13 12 11 10   7 6 5 4 3 2 1

Library of Congress Cataloging-in-Publication Data

Volf, Miroslav.

Against the tide: love in a time of petty dreams and persisting enmities /
Miroslav Volf.

p.   cm.

Essays originally published in The Christian century, 1996-2008.

ISBN 978-0-8028-6506-9 (pbk.: alk. paper)

1. Christian life. 2. Love — Religious aspects — Christianity.   I. Title.

BV4639.V6   2010

248.4 — dc22

2009040901

Note: With the exception of "All about Getting," the essays in this book are re-prints of articles originally published in *The Christian Century* from 1996 to 2008.

In memory of
Tomislav Simic

Contents

Family Matters

Church

Mission and Other Faiths

Culture and Politics

Giving and Forgiving

Hope and Reconciliation

Perspective

Introduction: Steps toward Love

It was February 2009, a few days after my return from the first International Chiefs of Military Chaplains Conference in Cape Town, South Africa. I had delivered a keynote address at the event and, thankful that it had been well received by chaplains from a broad range of faiths, proceeded to email the text of the speech to my friend, H.R.H. Prince Ghazi bin Muhammad. A few days later, I received his reply: "Very nice," he wrote, then added, "I notice all your stuff is characterized by 'systematic baby steps towards love.'"

Prince Ghazi himself is no stranger to thinking about love. As a young scholar at the University of Cambridge, he wrote his doctoral thesis on the literary archetype of "falling in love." More recently, he was the principal author of the widely endorsed Muslim document titled *A Common Word Between Us and You*, which focuses on the dual command to love God and love neighbor as "common ground" between Christians and Muslims. He is well aware that Christians tend to define God as "Love" — at least, to the extent that the incomprehensible One who "dwells in unapproachable light" (1 Timothy 6:16) can be defined at all. Yet I detected a note of mild surprise in his comment that "*all* my stuff" can be characterized by steps toward love, even "stuff" about the military and military chaplains.

Though I would not have put it the way Prince Ghazi did, I think he is basically correct — everything I write stems from one simple conviction: "God is love" (1 John 4:9). "Love" describes the very being of the eternal and self-subsisting God; and "love" describes all God's dealings with the temporal and contingent world, from its creation, through redemption, to consummation. The Christian Bible makes clear, in manifold ways, that, whatever else the world is, it is a theater of divine love — Love whose face shines on creatures; Love whose anger sometimes burns against their all-too-prevalent nastiness; Love who, divine anger notwithstanding, bears human sin and enmity so as to return us back to our original good. What is that original good? Created as we are in the image of the God who is love, we can live genuinely flourishing lives only when we also love — love God with all our being, and love our neighbors as ourselves. That is what Jesus taught as the first and most important commandments (Mark 12:29-31) and the fundamental framework for interpreting all of scripture (Matthew 22:40). That is what I strive for my theology to be all about. At its best, that is what Christian theology has been all about for centuries.

All the essays comprising this book urge Christians to reflect in our lives the love that God is. Whether I write about God or the self; about my sons, presidents and their advisors, or popes; whether I discuss churches, activist communities, or other religions; whether I analyze culture, business, or politics; whether I reflect about old enmities or new alliances, about past wrongs or future hopes, about joyful feasts or mournful funerals, everything in this book is about how to make determined steps toward love. As many have said, and as I hope will become plain from these essays, love is not a warm feeling — though warm feelings may accompany it. At its core, love is not a feeling at all, but an action, a way of being, in active care for others — for the integrity of their bodies and souls, as well as for their flourishing. For all the diversity of these essays, they are unified by a passion for active care, for love.

This book has another source of unity: all its essays call for Christians to live "against the tide." The obstacles to "Project Love" are formidable. Chief among them is our obvious and nearly universal propensity to care for ourselves alone, or to care for others only if the benefit to us outweighs the cost. It may be too strong to say that we are wired for selfishness; but it is astounding how easy it is for us — upstanding sons and daughters, husbands and wives, workers and leaders — to turn into what Philip Roth has called "black holes of self-absorption": manipulating, cheating, deceiving, and exploiting others — and all with a clear conscience.

That inner pull toward self-absorption and away from care for others is reinforced by what I have elsewhere called a "culture stripped of grace."* In this market-driven and market-saturated world in which we live, it makes less and less sense to give — to impart even a *tad* bit more than we expect in return. Instead, with the horizon of our hopes shrunk from the vastness of God's infinity to the narrowness of our own self's boundaries, we make every effort to get out of everything more than we put in. Indeed, we feel fully justified in making our own benefit and our own satisfaction the sole criteria for determining our actions. Similarly, as we strive to protect ourselves from the violence and injustice that surround and assault us, it makes less and less sense to forgive — to forgo a rightful claim against those who have wronged us. Instead, insisting zealously on the inviolability of our own rights, we seek retribution. In fact, often we don't stop at retribution but hunt down our violators like predatory beasts. These two ways in which our culture is stripped of grace are two sides of the same shiny but valueless coin of self-absorption; in both we demand more than is rightfully ours, rather than extending ourselves in generosity toward others.

In this book, love-as-care pushes in a wide variety of ways and settings against our bent toward easy pampering of self and stern retribution of others. However good it may feel in the moment, giving in to these tendencies is petty, unfulfilling, and destructive for individuals and, indeed, whole cultures. We are born for a higher calling, for a more satisfying pursuit, for more harmonious and sustainable lives. We are born to care, to engage in "Project Love."

Most of the essays in this book were previously published as columns in *The Christian Century.* I am grateful to the editors, above all David Heim and Debra Bendis, for providing me a stimulus to reflect and write about how the God of love intersects with the ordinary as well as the extraordinary in human lives, with the sausage-making Grandpa Djordje or the king-defying Sir Thomas More. Susan Richardson (early on) and Connie Gundry Tappy (in the final stages) have helped me craft a book out of those columns. I am thankful to them both.

---

* See Miroslav Volf, *Free of Charge: Giving and Forgiving in a Culture Stripped of Grace* (Grand Rapids: Zondervan, 2005).

GOD AND THE SELF

God's Delight

I have always been fascinated by the phrase "the Lord make his face shine upon you." God's blessing, God's protection, God's peace, God's grace — all part of that same benediction — are great goods, and if I had to choose between them and God's shining face, I might well opt for them. But God's shining face outdoes them all. For God's blessing, protection, peace, and grace concern things that we possess, do, and suffer, while God's shining face concerns our very being. It stands for God's sheer delight that we exist and live before him. Yet I rarely "see" God's face shining upon me, and given that, as all of us, I am an inveterate sinner, it is not easy to know exactly why God's face should shine on me.

I know what I am missing. My second son, Aaron, is a sweet little boy who loves to cuddle, to the point of hugging hardwood floors if his parents are not conveniently around. When I pick him up, he buries his head into my shoulder and holds tight around my neck. Then he suddenly lifts his head and looks me straight in the eyes, his face beaming with delight, and says "Tata" (Croatian for "daddy") for no other reason than that I am with him.

Aaron delights in me partly because he does not remember my transgressions against him and does not know in advance all the future strains on our relationship. But could we imagine God as a child, in blissful forgetfulness of what was and in naïve ignorance of what is to come? What would happen to Aaron's shining face if, when he looked me in the eyes, he could remember a big daddy hand pulling him away from the joy of scattering plant dirt all over the oriental rugs? What if he could, somewhere in the future, catch a glimpse of daddy's mighty frustration descending upon him for no reason other than that he happened to be there? Unlike Aaron, God knows the past, present, and future, and his gaze penetrates below all surfaces to the dark chambers of our deceitful hearts. We are all sinners. How then can God delight in us?

Am I forgetting that God is love? No, I am not. God loves all prodigal daughters and sons, notwithstanding our ever-present sin against God and neighbors. But is the love of prodigals a love that *delights*? It is the kind of love committed to the well-being of the beloved, love that suffers pain at the beloved's journey into the far country, love that wants the beloved to return as a true lover. Would it not be in some sense even wrong for God to delight in the wrongdoer? Is not distance between us and God — God's anger and our terror of it — appropriate as long as we remain prodigals? Is this not what the prophet Isaiah felt when he exclaimed, "Woe is me! I am lost, for I am a man of unclean lips . . . yet my eyes have seen the King, the Lord of hosts!"?

Why is it that we think that God should delight in us when we act — and in an important sense also are — contrary to God, the source of all goodness, truth, and beauty? Is not longing for God's shining face just an echo of the infantile desire to be affirmed no matter what — a desire so pervasive in our culture that we cannot imagine how anyone could disapprove of something we do and still love us? Should we not rather live content with God's frowning face, knowing well that God's condemnation of sin is a form God's love must take if the sinner is to be redeemed? Should we not grow up, face the truth about ourselves, learn to live with God's disapproval, and find comfort in God's love out of which this disapproval is born? God's shining face would then be a promise for the world to come, where God would have nothing to disapprove of and we would rest in God's eternal delight.

But that can be only partly right. The priestly benediction is given for the here and now, not for the then and there. It speaks of a God who can make God's face shine on people in the midst of the darkness of their sin. But how can that be? How can God's face shine on a sinful creature? Miracle of miracles, it turns out that God is not completely unlike my toddler son in the moment when his face shines upon mine. What does the forgiving God do with our sins? Here is what the scripture says: God covers them, God disperses them like mist, God puts them behind his back,

God hides them, God forgets them. As Søren Kierkegaard puts it in *Works of Love:* "The one who loves forgives in this way: he forgives, he forgets, he blots out the sin, in love he turns toward the one he forgives; but when he turns toward him, he of course cannot see what is lying behind his back."

Difficulties abound. Is it possible for the all-knowing God not to see certain things? How can God both see so as to condemn sin, and not see so as to delight in the forgiven one? Can God switch off realms of knowledge at will? These are tough philosophical and theological questions with no easy answers, and this is no place to enter the debate. But I can make one general suggestion for those who want to worship the God of Abraham and Sarah: If you have a notion of God that precludes the shining of God's face on a sinner, you should give up that notion and bask in God's shining face.

You Can't Deal with God

As I was writing this piece, Good Friday was in view, and I thought of the renowned Viennese composer Antonio Salieri as portrayed in the movie *Amadeus*. In a scene from Salieri's childhood, Salieri is kneeling before a crucifix and trying to make a bargain with God. "Lord, make me a great composer! Let me celebrate your glory through music — and be celebrated myself. Make me famous throughout the world, dear God! Make me immortal!" What will God get for doing him the favor? "In return," says Salieri, "I vow I will give you my chastity — my industry, my deepest humility, every hour of my life. And I will help my fellow man all I can." Salieri is offering God a deal: I'll sacrifice for you, and in return you'll fulfill my desire for immortal glory.

Why did Salieri think that God would consider such a proposition? Because, like many of us, he must have believed that God is a negotiator. "If I do this, God will give me that" in the mouth of a human being is the obverse of "If you do this, I'll give you that" in the mouth of God. God demands, and if we do what God demands, then God gives. Or we offer to do God a favor, and God rewards us with things we desire. This is the way God is, such reasoning goes. God is basically a negotiator.

If God were basically a negotiator, human beings would always end up with a raw deal. For one thing, God doesn't need anything we have to offer. God can walk away from any proposition. And as any negotiator knows, it is impossible to strike a good deal under such conditions. When Salieri offers God his chastity, industry, and humility in return for musical genius, God can tell him, "I've got something you want, but you've got nothing I need," and then proceed to give musical genius to

Salieri's nemesis, a young brat by the name of Mozart. Second, even if we could entice God into making a deal with us, we would have no way of enforcing compliance. Since God doesn't need anything and God's power infinitely exceeds ours, God can break any contract — contracts are legitimately breakable — give us a bit of cash as compensation, and leave us out in the cold.

All this holds true if we are the ones trying to obtain something from God — if it is we who say, "I'll give you this [devotion] in exchange for that [musical genius]." But long before we thought of offering anything to God, God made demands on us, and these demands are awfully hard to fulfill. The law of Moses as expressed in the Ten Commandments was a heavy burden for the people of Israel. Even though God gave the law to them for their well-being, it proved to be too difficult to fulfill.

If we see the God of Jesus Christ as a negotiator, we'll experience the law of Christ as an even heavier burden than the law of Moses. In the Sermon on the Mount, for example, Christ intensifies Old Testament commands and interprets them to refer to inner states, not just outward acts. The prohibition against murder is intensified into the command not to be angry (Matt. 5:21-23); the prohibition against adultery becomes the command not to lust (Matt. 5:27-30); the command to love one's neighbor is expanded to include the command to love one's enemies (Matt. 5:43-47). Even tougher than the Ten Commandments is Jesus' insistence that we be nothing less than "perfect as your heavenly Father is perfect" (Matt. 5:48) — clearly an impossibility for mere humans! And yet if God were a negotiator, we would have to be divinely perfect before we could receive anything from God.

It is true that the scripture portrays God relating to people in ways remarkably similar to the image of God the negotiator. In the Old Testament we read, for instance, "If you will only obey the LORD your God . . . all these blessings shall come upon you and overtake you, if you obey the LORD your God" (Deut. 28:1-2). Yet the God of scripture is not a negotiator God. Before God gave commandments to the people of Israel, God delivered them from slavery in Egypt. Why? To get something out of them? No. God delivered them for the simple reason that God had heard their cry of affliction, kept the promises made to their ancestor Abraham, and, through deliverance and faithfulness, wanted to manifest divine glory in the world. Why did God give the commandments to the people he delivered? To gain their obedience so as to be able to reward them in return? The commandments themselves are rewards, given not for God's sake but for the sake of people's well-being (see Deut. 10:13).

In *Amadeus,* Salieri ends up a bitter old man, angry at God, angry at the world, angry at himself — to the point of attempting to take his own life. The entire course of his life rested on the deal he thought he'd made with God. God proved to be, as he put it, "wicked," in giving him "thirty-two years of meaningless fame" only to thrust him into permanent oblivion. But in fact no deal had been made between them. Salieri had made a proposition to God as he was kneeling at the cross, but God didn't take him up on it. Why? Because God hanging on the cross for the salvation of the world is not a negotiating God. On the cross, God is not setting up the terms of a contract that humanity needs to fulfill. God isn't saying: "I died for you, now you've got to do what I tell you to do." Instead, God is giving God's own self so that humanity may have life, and life abundant. God is not a negotiator. God is a giver.

Freed from Selfhood

As I was browsing through a used bookstore, I chanced upon a small treasure, an early English translation of a book whose author we don't know (identified only by place of residence, as "the Frankfurter"). I could only guess at the date of composition (probably toward the end of the fourteenth century). The nondescript title — *Theologia Germanica* — was chosen by someone other than the author. Martin Luther, the great Protestant reformer, was the first to publish the book in 1516, mainly because he had "not seen a more wholesome theology, one more in accordance with the Gospels, either in Latin or in our language." In the preface to the second edition he praised the author, who spoke "beyond the manner of ordinary preachers and teachers.... Yea, [the book] floats not on the surface like foam on the water, but it is gathered from the bottom of the Jordan by a true Israelite, whose name God knows."

Contemporary cultural sensibilities would likely predispose a Western reader to disagree with Luther about the wholesomeness of the book's theology. Its opening lines seem both pretentious and quaint: "Here begins the Frankfurter and speaks very lofty and lovely things concerning a perfect life. Jesus. Mary. John." But the real problem lies in the way the book treats the human self. Whereas we believe that we should unreservedly affirm the self, the *Theologia Germanica* argues that we should radically deny it. "A man should stand and be so free from himself, that is, from selfhood, I-hood, Me, Mine and the like, that in all things he should no more seek and regard himself and his own than if he did not exist, and should take as little account of himself as if he were not and another had done all his works." For "I-hood, selfhood,

Mine, Me and the like, all belong to the Devil, and therefore it is, that he is an evil Spirit."

"Has not the denial of the self become so radical here," we may protest, "that it undermines the plausibility of the position taken? Does not the I end up obliterated? Have not human beings here been dragged down to the level of mere sentient beings without self-consciousness?" But the *Theologia Germanica* is careful not to cross that line. For in that case God could neither be desired nor loved, and human beings would be "as the brutes that have no reason." The goal is not the erasure of the self but its preparation to become "nothing else but a house and habitation of God." And just why should we strive after this goal? The reason the book gives is as simple as it is profound: "Now that creature in which the Eternal Good most manifests itself, shines forth, works, is most known and loved, is the best, and that where in the Eternal Good least manifests itself is the least good of all creatures."

A basic principle of the *Theologia Germanica* is: "The more God indwells me, the better I am as a human being." A basic principle of contemporary Western culture, on the other hand, is: "The more I possess — the more power, the more 'toys,' the more pleasure — the better I am as a human being." It might seem that contemporary culture would do a better job helping the self to thrive than would the *Theologia Germanica*. Yet this is not so.

Consider sex in relation to our belief that the only duties and rights that matter "are those which indulge the self." Freed from the shackles of what is deemed repressive morality, the modern self seeks guiltless erotic pleasure whenever and wherever he or she can find it. Has that self therefore become sexually fulfilled? As Adam Kirsch points out in his review of Frank Bidard's *Desire*, "We value sexual desire so highly that we do not want it to refer beyond itself." As a consequence, we are incapable of seeing sexual pleasure as a sacrament for something more enduring. Sex therefore gets reduced to "the neurological effects of vascular congestion in the genitals," as one critic put it. Far from finding fulfillment, the self turned in upon itself loses itself in the emptiness of its own meaninglessness. And the emptier the self is, the more obsessed with the self we become; and the more obsessed with the self we are, the emptier the self becomes.

Our obsession with the self is equal in wisdom to the act of shooting oneself in the foot. But more than being just foolish, this obsession of the self with itself is also petty. Think of the author of the *Theologia Germanica*. She — or was it a he? — wanted for the self nothing less than to make it a habitation of God, that perfect existence "which comprehends and includes all existences in Itself and in Its Essence; and without which and beside which, there is no true being; and in which all things have their life. For It is the Essence of all things and is in Itself unchangeable and immovable, yet It changes and moves all things else." Directed completely away from itself toward God, the self of the *Theologia Germanica* finds itself host to the source and goal of all being. Surely a rather immodest "accomplishment" for a self that is intent on being free "from selfhood, I-hood, Me, Mine and the like"!

Scaling a Sandy Slope

"Incredible wealth" and "breathless pace" — two of the most prominent features of Western societies as the old millennium ended and
the new began. True, it is breathless pace for all, and incredible wealth
only for some. Yet the eyes of all are set on material wealth, and so we
keep running. Faster and faster. In his classic *The Affluent Society*, John
Kenneth Galbraith compared the struggle in modern societies to satisfy
wants with the "efforts of the squirrel to keep abreast of the wheel that is
propelled by his own efforts." We work in order to spend and we spend in
order to work; the faster we work the more we spend, and the more we
spend the faster we must work. "If you want to have more cake tomorrow, you have to eat more today." This counterintuitive wisdom of today's
economic life has become a basic rule for the way we live. And if anyone
asks, "Why would one want to eat so much cake in the first place?" we
give her a look of surprised incomprehension.

One day I was leafing through a new volume in *The Complete Works
of Friedrich Nietzsche.* In one of his early unpublished writings, Nietzsche
observed his contemporaries' obsession with power, glory, and money-
making. If we give our world a good look, he claimed, we will see "refined
beasts of prey run, and we [ourselves] run[ning] in their midst." He continued:

> The tremendous mobility of human beings on the great earthly desert,
> their founding of cities and states, their waging of wars, their ceaseless
> gathering and dispersing, their confused mingling, their imitation and
> deceit of one another, their mutual outwitting and trampling under-

foot, their cries in distress and their joyous cheers in victory — all this is a continuation of animality, as if human beings were intended to regress and be cheated out of their metaphysical disposition; indeed, as if nature, having yearned and labored for human beings for so long, now recoiled from them in fear and preferred to return to the unconsciousness of instinct.

The bait with which human beings have been lured into slavery to their inane desires, says Nietzsche, is "earthly happiness." And the veil they hang "over the vulgar and animalistic face of a wild lust for existence" in order to hide its true nature from themselves is a "culture of luxury" — "the rich and powerful human being, a free personality, the cultured state."

The slippage into animality is neither human fate nor a result of the mindlessness of consumers or the deviousness of producers, argued Nietzsche. It is rather a strategy of evasion.

Everyone knows from his own experience how unpleasant memories suddenly force themselves upon us and how we then make an effort to drive them out of our heads by means of violent gestures and sounds — but the general structure of our life indicates that we always find ourselves in such a state: What is it that assails us so often, what mosquito is this that refuses to let us sleep?

In this fragmentary text, Nietzsche does not tell us what it is that disturbs our rest and what troubling message it seeks to whisper into our ears. The only clue we get is a mysterious reference to our "metaphysical disposition" that nudges us to elevate our "gaze beyond the horizon of the animal."

The idea of a human "metaphysical disposition" led my thought back across the centuries to Gregory of Nyssa, whom I read in preparation for teaching a class on eschatology. Gregory contrasts the true progress of a soul who seeks the infinite God with the seeming progress of a soul oriented toward finite things. The latter is "like those who scale a sandy slope. Even if they look like they are traversing great tracts of ground on foot, they tire themselves to no avail. Each time the sand slides to the bottom, in such a way that there is a great effort of movement but not progress."

To use a different metaphor, those who merely seek sensual pleasures, material possessions, or earthly glory are like children whose carefully crafted sandcastles are washed by the waves, like beasts that go in circles with eyes blinkered and necks tethered to the millstone of this life. If human beings seek to hold onto things that are dissolving and flowing away from them, they will end up "swept away by the current of what is unstable."

The only proper object of human desires is the inexhaustible richness of the eternal God. As Hans Urs von Balthasar puts it in *Presence and Thought,* for Gregory, the created spirit is meant to realize that "paradoxical synthesis of a desire that can only grow in joy, because the infinity of the object loved increases and rejuvenates in it for all eternity an impetus that tends toward an end that cannot be attained." If Gregory is right, it could be that the "mosquito . . . that refuses to let us sleep" and that we are trying to drive away with our frantic activity is none other than the divine Spirit telling us that our ultimate fulfillment is only in the mystery of the infinite God.

Ludwig Feuerbach famously suggested that we project our worldly ideals onto God and then worship them; God's infinity is the reverse side of human insatiability. But I suspect that we are involved in an inverse projection, by which we infuse the works of our own hands with the spurious ability to satisfy our hunger for the infinite God. The endless stream of new goods and services that keeps us running at "breathless pace" has become for us a cornucopia of mystery, protection, and salvation. It looks utterly worldly, and yet inscribed all over it is a misdirected desire for God.

Can We Be Good without God?

Some have suggested that recent scandals in the world of business, politics, and the academy are practical consequences of a worldview that has pushed God out. Morality needs God, the argument goes, and without God the social fabric will be torn by uncontrolled greed, lust for power, and striving for glory.

Clearly, however, you can also have a good deal of "immorality" even if God occupies a central place in your worldview. Scandals in the religious communities are proof of this, if proof is needed. Moreover, convictions about God sometimes explicitly underwrite morally reprehensible acts, as when greed and violence get justified on religious grounds. What should we conclude from the fact that those who believe in God both do evil and legitimize their deeds by belief in God? Only that belief in God is compatible with "immoral" life, not that morality does not need God.

But does morality need God? A fine and accessible book on the subject is *Why Bother Being Good? The Place of God in the Moral Life,* by John Hare, professor of philosophy at Calvin College. He is one of the most important Christian moral philosophers writing today (see *The Moral Gap* and *God's Call*). He argues powerfully that morality does need God. His point is not that a person who doesn't believe in God can't be good — there are many such people, and some of them live lives worthy of saints. The morally rigorous eighteenth-century philosopher Immanuel Kant considered seventeenth-century Jewish rationalist philosopher Baruch Spinoza to be such a person. But because saintly atheists live better than they believe, says Hare, they lack some essential beliefs that sustain the kind of life they lead. They cannot make sense of their own moral lives.

15

One standard way to argue that morality needs God is to show that we must make an appeal to God if we want to give an adequate answer to the question, "Why should we be good?" In the second half of his book, Hare offers a version of such an argument, mainly by discarding the available alternatives as inadequate. The authority of morality is not just obvious, and it is not grounded in the demands of reason. Moreover, it cannot come from the need to be true either to our human nature or to the community to which we belong. It would take too long to give Hare's reasons for discarding these ways of construing why we should be good. But by using the process of elimination, Hare is able to argue that the authority of morality can come only from God's will and God's call.

Often people who argue that morality needs God stop after showing that God is the only adequate source of morality's authority. Hare does not. God is relevant not only to why we should be good, but also to how we *can* be good. Our ability is indeed a problem. All of us experience a demand for a morality that is "too high for us given the natural capacities we are born with." We try various strategies to help ourselves out, such as "puffing up our capacity" or "reducing the demand." But these are clearly futile, argues Hare, for our natural capacity remains hopelessly limited and the demand inescapably high.

To be able to be moral we need "moral faith: . . . the faith that it is possible for us to be morally good in our hearts and the faith that the world outside us makes moral sense." Moral people have to believe both that "their capacities have been transformed inside themselves" and that "the world outside is the kind of place in which happiness is reliably connected with a morally good life."

A different way of putting this second condition is simply to say that "moral people need to believe that they do not have to do what is morally bad to be happy." The point seems well taken: if we are persuaded that we cannot satisfy the demands of morality and that we will be miserable when we do, we are not likely to try to be moral. Hare argues that the "moral faith" necessary for leading moral lives demands faith in God — the one who can transform hearts and providentially leads the world in such a way that (in the end) virtue will unite with happiness.

So are we back to the claim that one cannot lead a moral life if one does not *believe* in God? Not quite. For whether we believe in God or not,

God may be at work in the hearts of people and in the providential leading of the world. But if Hare is right, then the "morality we are familiar with requires a theological background if it is going to make sense." This does not prove that theological doctrines are true. It shows that "if we want to hang on to this morality and reject the theology, then we will have to find some substitute to do the work that the theology used to do. It is not going to be easy to find such a substitute."

In the face of the scandals that have shaken the confidence of people in business, government, academia, and religious communities, leaders of the Christian churches often take on the mantle of critics who complain about the state of the "world" and, less frequently, the mantle of reformers who offer ways to improve it. If Hare is right, they should not neglect their primary task of witnessing to the God of Jesus Christ. For we must appeal to God to answer two central questions that lie at the heart of any moral crisis: "Why should we be morally good?" and "How can we be morally good?"

Dancing for God

I wasn't sure what to make of *Frida,* a movie about the sadness, courage, and indomitability that characterized the life of Mexican painter Frida Kahlo. Because I wanted to know more, I watched the interview Bill Moyers did with the movie's director, Julie Taymor. I went away from their interchange with a fresh perspective on artistic creation — and a fresh perspective on how pastors and theologians do theology.

Toward the end of the interview, Taymor tells of her visit to Bali many years ago as a young artist. One day she was alone in a secluded wooded area at the edge of a clearing, quietly listening to the distant music of indigenous celebrations. Suddenly, into the clearing came thirty or forty old men dressed in the full splendor of warrior costumes and each carrying a spear. They started to dance, and Taymor, who was hidden by the deep shadows of trees, observed them for what seemed an eternity. Then she had an epiphany of sorts:

> . . . they danced to nobody. They were performing for God. . . . They did not care if someone was paying for tickets, writing reviews, they did not care if an audience was watching, they did it from the inside to the outside and from the outside in, and that profoundly moved me. . . .

To Taymor, these dancing warriors became symbols of noncommercialized art, art guided by the artist's inner vision rather than art held captive to the sensibilities of its potential audiences. To her, they stood for an authenticity unspoiled by the desire for popularity. To me, they became symbols of theology undertaken above all for the sake of God and under the judgment of God.

You may think that ministers and theologians should not need to be reminded that God is their primary audience. After all, theology's main subject is the living God, creator, redeemer, and consummator of the world. What ought to matter to them more than anything else is what God might think of their work. Yet more often than not as we speak or write, we think to ourselves: "What will our colleagues or parishioners say? How will this or that interest group react? How spirited or how long will the applause be? How will our book do on the amazon.com list? Will it get this or that award?" We speak and write to get approval from an audience, to impress reviewers, to satisfy "customers."

If we continue down this road, soon we will be preaching and theologizing the way some of our elected officials govern: mainly by polling the preferences of their constituencies and then acting accordingly. Popularity and its rewards will take precedence over fidelity to God. We will perform for audiences instead of dancing for God. In the process, we will morph into the image of those we seek to please.

But doesn't "dancing for God" sound too pious? Doesn't the idea suggest a basic mistake about the nature of theology and ministry generally? Presumably the purpose of theology is to be helpful to the world, not to God. God doesn't need theology; if anybody needs it, it is the world. How can one communicate effectively without taking into account the needs and sensibilities, linguistic habits, and cultural and personal preferences of the people for whom one is theologizing? Theology and ministry in this regard is not like prayer. Hypocrites love to stand and pray in public places so that they may be seen by others; true followers of Christ, Jesus taught, go to their rooms, shut their doors, and pray in secret. You should pray the way those Balinese old men danced — with no human eye watching. But you should not do theology like that. When you pray, you speak to God; when you theologize, you speak to fellow human beings.

There is a major difference between Taymor's dancers and theologians. Unlike those dancers, theologians essentially speak to people. We interpret the world to them in the light of God's designs; we reflect on how to align our lives and our world with God's purposes. Both what we say and how we put it cannot be just a matter of movement "from the in-

19

side to the outside," to use Taymor's phrase. We are pastors, and we must be sensitive to the specific needs and situations of our parish. Neither in the way we speak nor in the content of our speaking and writing can we abstract from all audiences and have only God on our minds.

Yet the analogy to Balinese dancers applies too. *As* we are speaking and writing for our fellow human beings, we are dancing for God. A god for whom you can dance only when you are not dancing for people must be a false god — a god shut up in his own sphere pursuing his own interests unrelated to the well-being of people. But this is not who the Father of Jesus Christ is. God is the creator and a lover of creation; God's sphere and interests include human beings and their world. It is impossible to dance *for* this God to the *detriment* of creation because a dance pleasing to God confers *blessing* upon creation. Put another way, only a dance that pleases God will confer blessing on creation.

A few months ago, I was on a spiritual retreat in the hills of Vermont. At the end of the retreat we participants prayed for one another. I will never forget a simple prayer a musician offered for me. He asked God that as a theologian I would "play to the audience of One." Although I had heard the phrase before, was deeply attracted to the notion and at the same time frightened by it. Do I have the courage, I wondered, to play as though God, the lover of creation, were the only one listening? Unless I do, my fear and timidity will be revealed as a failure to trust and love God as well as to properly serve God's creatures.

The Reality of Evil
and the Possibility of Hope

Evil and Evildoers

"**N**othing is gained and much is lost if we describe the terrorists as evil," a friend of mine argued recently. I disagree. Our difference can be traced back to a division in moral philosophy. My friend is a moral expressivist. He views moral judgments as expressions of feelings, desires, and wants. We add nothing to the description of the situation, he says, when we name our enemies as evil. Instead, we should state what we feel about them and their acts, and what we intend to do in response.

I, on the other hand, count myself among the moral realists. Moral realists emphasize the reality of value properties, such as moral goodness or moral evil. If we drop words like "good" and "evil" from our vocabulary, say the realists, we seriously misperceive the character of some acts and abandon the relations between human beings to the play of power.

My friend's and my difference in moral philosophy goes hand in hand with our disagreement about human nature. Humans are good and rational, my friend argues, and we insult humanity if we call some of its members evil. He prefers to explain their "evil" acts by pernicious influences — a set of nasty genes, abusive parents, unjust structures, manipulative leaders. I agree to a point. But there is no greater insult to a human being than to reduce her to a set of influences. Our condemnation of her deed notwithstanding, we *respect* an evildoer by calling her evil because we are treating her as a responsible being.

My friend and I also disagree about what we mean when we call someone evil and about how we should treat "evildoers." He says that calling Osama bin Laden "evil" conjures up an image of evil incarnate.

"Think of the phrase 'we have seen the face of evil,'" he says. "It suggests that bin Laden is nothing but wickedness."

"That may be what people mean when they call a particularly vile person 'evil,' but that is not what the Christian tradition means," I respond. The essence of evil is negation of the good. But it is a cardinal mistake to equate an evil person with evil itself, even in the case of the devil and his demonic hosts. There are no beings who are pure evil. Because evil is negation of good — privation, theologians would say — it lives off the good. One can be evil only if one is partly good. If one were to do the impossible by becoming pure evil, one would simply cease to be. To say that bin Laden is evil is precisely not to say that he is evil incarnate (or it is to say that as soon as evil becomes incarnate, it has ceased to be pure). He remains God's good creature who pursues undeniable goods even as he does evil.

We underestimate an evildoer if we understand him as "a shape-shifting demon, a wild-card moral anarchist beyond our comprehension," as Stanley Fish recently stated. Evildoers are dangerous to more than just themselves precisely because in their evil schemes they are pursuing important goods, for themselves and for their communities. A person can be successfully evil only if he or she can embody a peculiarly nasty blend of vicious evil and laudable good.

My friend's worry about calling a person evil has an obverse. "Describing bin Laden as evil serves only to underscore our own goodness," he argues. I can see why he is worried, especially with his understanding of what it means to be evil. If a person is evil incarnate, then he is qualitatively different from the rest of us. He is evil itself; we are good, with some admixture of evil.

"In my view," I tell him, "bin Laden remains a good creature of God, his evil notwithstanding. There is no *qualitative* difference between him and any of us. Most of us may not be as evil as he is, but we are evil in the same sense that he is. Even at our best, the scripture teaches, we are not pure goodness; our most lofty ideals are tainted by evil." There is reason to worry, I admit, even if one believes that the difference between bin Laden and the rest of us is quantitative, not qualitative. We are prone to take his great evil as a sign of our goodness. This is a foolish thing to do, of course. I have not improved morally even a tiniest bit when someone else has deteriorated morally. However, vain as we are, we seem not to mind being foolish if we can feel superior.

But this is no reason to forgo describing egregious perpetrators as "evil." Instead, our propensity to delight in our own goodness when others are described as evil is a form of sin — a sin of convenient falsehood and pride.

"Doesn't calling a person 'evil' make us go after him with a vengeance, seeking to eliminate or at least neutralize him?" my friend protests. "It all too often does," I agree. But it *should* not. God's love is broad enough to include evildoers, the worst of them. We know this because Christ died for their salvation no less than for the salvation of the rest of us who are one and all by nature God's enemies. To call someone evil is not to place her beyond the pale of God's redemption. Similarly, to call her evil is not to exempt ourselves from the obligation to love her. If our enemies are hungry, we should feed them; if they are thirsty, we should give them something to drink. Instead of being overcome by evil, we should overcome evil with good.

I worry when I hear politicians speak of bin Laden as the Evil One Who Hides. But I would worry even more if we were to refrain from naming morally reprehensible acts, and those who commit them, as evil.

Demons or Evildoers?

"I want to make a case for demonizing the perpetrator!" The comment, "only partly facetious," came in response to a lecture I had just delivered on the implications of the story of Cain and Abel for our relation to victims and criminals. I had noted "a pervasive cultural obsession with criminals and a rather quick forgetfulness of victims and their families" and observed that, in contrast, the story of Cain and Abel "takes decidedly the perspective of the victim and condemns the perpetrator." At the same time, "the story underscores the imperative that we not demonize the perpetrator."

"I know what you mean by that," said my disagreeing friend, "especially what you mean by that individually and pastorally. But in the public realm, that phrase often implies a mushy, maudlin, wimpish sort of 'what they did really wasn't wrong' and 'they aren't evil' kind of attitude common among a lot of politicians in this town [Washington]."

Never mind that immediately after my plea not to demonize the perpetrator I added, "True, justice must be pursued, and the punishment of the criminals may be appropriate. But even at their worst, criminals remain human beings and are therefore 'neighbors' for whom we must care." My interlocutor was afraid that I failed to recognize the radical nature of evil and was in danger of going soft on crime. A bit of "demonizing," he thought, would remedy the situation.

I protested, of course. No, I was not talking simply "individually" or "pastorally." I meant that we should abstain from demonizing in public discourse, especially there. In former Yugoslavia or Rwanda, just as in Hitler's Germany — or, for that matter, throughout the history of the

United States — before the others were excluded they were showered with a barrage of "dysphemisms"; they were called "vermin," "beasts," or "demons."

The language of dehumanization legitimized the practice of oppression, even extermination. And no, I did not think that "dehumanizing the perpetrators" was a good way to retrieve the talk about evil in the public realm. To the contrary, it is a sign that we have lost the ability to name evil and have taken a wrong turn in fighting it, a turn deeply at odds with the inner logic of the Christian faith.

We stutter when it comes to evil. Andrew Delbanco's *The Death of Satan* — on the whole, not a profound book — starts with the following astute observation, "A gulf has opened up in our culture between the visibility of evil and the intellectual resources available for coping with it. Never before have images of horror been so widely disseminated and so appalling. . . . Yet never have our responses been so weak. We have no language for connecting our inner lives with the horrors that pass before our eyes in the outer world."

Why do words fail us when it comes to naming evil? Partly, it is because evil is irrational. Its "reasons" lie hidden in the impenetrable regions of human hearts, where wills feed on proclivities and proclivities are shaped by wills, and where both proclivities and wills react in unpredictable ways to what our neighbors, our culture, and social systems we inhabit do to us. Up against the irrationality of evil, our language spins like the tires of a car stuck in the snow: evil is evil is evil is evil. . . .

Another reason why words fail us when it comes to evil is that we in the West today hesitate to ascribe evil to human beings. It is below their dignity, we think. Human beings are basically good and therefore incapable of truly evil acts. If they act in an evil way, we search for explanations — in their bodily make-up, family, economic status, culture. If told that a person chose evil, we strain ourselves to peek behind the choice and discover its "mechanism." Riding smoothly on good explanations, we find ourselves in a land where our hearts tremble at the sight of obvious evil, but our minds will not recognize evil as evil or the one who did it as an evildoer. To help ourselves out, we "demonize."

Notice two things that happen when we fail to identify evil simply as evil, a terrible and culpable but basically human evil, and when we fail to call the person who committed it an "evildoer." First, we must dehumanize the perpetrators. To take seriously the evil we cannot ascribe to them, we subtract from their humanity by demonizing or bestializing them. We affirm the putative basic goodness of humanity in general only to deny humanness to its members who do terrible deeds.

Second, we can have none but an adversarial relation to the perpetrators. If I call you "a demon," I'll punish you, lock you up, drive you away, exterminate you, but I will not treat you as an enemy I ought to love even as I fight your enmity, and I will not see you as a neighbor for whom I ought to care even as I relentlessly pursue justice for the victims.

To love you as an evildoer, I must see your evil as a human evil, rooted in your possibilities as a human being. In a strange way, it is a good thing to be able to call someone evil — provided that person *is* evil and that the one doing the calling is committed to loving the evildoer.

Washing Away and Washing Up

I saw my wife cringe the first time she read the children's book *Noah's Ark* to our son Nathanael. "A long time ago there lived a man called Noah. Noah was a good man, who trusted in God. There were also many wicked people in the world. God wanted to punish the wicked people, so he said to Noah, 'I shall make a flood of water and wash all the wicked people away.'" On the slight grimace which appeared on her face as she read about "washing people away" was written: "How destructive and cruel of God! How inappropriate to expose a toddler to such violence!"

In Nathanael's growing library, an alternative was available to what seemed like an account of divine "global cleansing." *The Greedy Python* is about a giant snake with a monstrous appetite who gobbled up all the animals, from mouse to elephant, and then coughed them up again because he felt too sick afterward. But, the story ends, "He hadn't learned a single thing: His greed was quite astonishing. He saw his own tail, long and curved, and thought that lunch was being served. He closed his jaws on his own rear, then swallowed hard . . . and disappeared!"

Now there, you may think, is a story about victory over evil that you can read to your children without offending your own moral sensibilities and assaulting their innocence. Evil implodes on itself and self-destructs. What is more, the convenient idea has the backing of some respectable biblical scholars. Commenting on the proper understanding of God's wrath, one of them has argued: "For Paul the impersonal character of the wrath [of God] was important; it relieved him of the necessity of attributing wrath directly to God, it transformed the wrath from an attribute of God into the name for a process which sinners bring upon themselves." As it turns out, however, biblical scholars who make this argument are plain wrong. In Paul, as in the rest of the Bible, wrath is not impersonal, but clearly has its origin in God (cf. Rom. 3:5; 9:22; 12:19). Indeed, Paul's central claims that God "justifies the ungodly" (Rom. 4:5) and that we were reconciled to God "while we were enemies" (Rom. 5:10), which seem incompatible with God's wrath, in fact presuppose it.

Reconciliation and justification do not issue from some mushy sentiment that, in the face of evil, shrugs the shoulders and turns a blind eye. Reconciliation is not "inclusion" of the enemy; justification is not "acceptance" of injustice and of the unjust. Essential for reconciliation and justification is the twin belief that (1) restoration of communion with the evildoer does not rest (cannot rest!) simply on the justice done but that (2) evil must be condemned and overcome. For Paul, God's unconditional grace toward sinners is unthinkable without judgment. A God of most radical grace must be a God of wrath — not the kind of wrath that burns against evildoers until they prove worthy of being loved, but the kind that resists evildoers because they are unconditionally loved.

Paul was wise not to share the "greedy python" account of evil's destiny. True, after a certain threshold has been reached, the purer the evil is, the less chance it has to survive. But evil is so pervasive precisely because evildoers know well how to pull back from evil so as not to destroy themselves; they even know how to be sufficiently "good" so as to thrive. Believing in the self-destruction of evil is a dangerous ideology. Evil will not take care of itself; it must be fought every step of the way.

And this is where God's wrath comes in. For God's wrath is nothing but God's stance of active opposition to evil. God is not "a nice guy in the sky," because evil is a cat with ten thousand lives. The God who would not oppose evil would be an indifferent demon who would condemn men and women to the power of evil's destructiveness. To tell Nathanael that the greedy python will devour himself is to tell him a soothing but morally dangerous lie. To tell him that God's anger burns against wickedness is to tell him a disturbing but morally transforming truth.

And yet, the story about God who decided to wash all the wicked people away had to be resisted. The next time Nathanael sat in his mother's lap and picked up *Noah's Ark,* the story was edited to read: "I shall make a flood of water and wash *up* all the wicked people." Had the bourgeois sensibilities and the need to protect his presumed innocence gotten the better of her? No. She was reading that story in the light of the many stories that followed it in the great narrative of salvation. More specifically, she connected the story with the sacrament of baptism, as the New Testament itself does (1 Pet. 3:20-21). As the waters of the great flood washed away the wicked people, so the waters of baptism close upon the baptized person to put the "old person" to death. But like Noah and his family who were saved by the ark, the baptized one emerges out of judgment into a new life by the power of Christ's resurrection.

Like the story of Noah, baptism contains a powerful divine "No" to human sinfulness, but it is a "No" enveloped in a divine "Yes," a "Yes" stronger than sin and death. Arguably, the story of Noah itself aims at some such divine "Yes." For it ends with the promise: "Nor shall I ever again destroy every living creature as I have done." And so God decided to wash up the wicked people.

Taking God to Court

In *Joseph and His Brothers,* Thomas Mann tells of an exchange between Jacob, who has just seen what he believes is proof of his son's death, and his servant Eliezer. The passage reminds me of two friends who were complaining about God.

"Yes, I acknowledge him, that terrible God," said one friend in a muted voice full of pent-up anger. "But God is my enemy. He refuses to do what even the worst of friends would gladly do. A small miracle to alleviate my pain and remove my humiliation would cost the Mighty One nothing. But he is deaf to my prayers. I'll fight him to keep my dignity, even if I lose my life."

"I despise God, that self-obsessed Lord of Lords," said the other friend, trying to shake loose of the One to whom she was still clinging, even in her anger. "On Friday evenings, God would just sit there in heavenly glory, soaking in all the praise that my mother and her fellow believers showered on him in church, while back at home my uncle was molesting me."

I understood perfectly well the rage of my friends; I sensed it welling up within me too. The dissonance between the belief in a mighty and loving God and the experience of unnecessary and unremedied suffering is too shrill to the soul's ear not to demand a resolution. In the absence of harmony, rage and rebellion reign. What my friends wanted from me, a theologian, was an acknowledgment of their pain and rebellion. And I gave it.

There would be no need for theology, however, if its task were merely to empathize with what people feel and to echo what they say about God. Rogerian therapy, say, would suffice. Theology's purpose is to help people speak rightly about God. After I expressed my genuine sympathy, I therefore added a "but." I gently challenged not their experiences but their claims about God's indifference and self-obsession. Predictably, my friends rebelled against my correction with even greater force than they had rebelled against God. I found myself cast in the image of Eliezer, the defender of God in Mann's story.

Eliezer warns the bereaved Jacob, who is accusing God of bad faith, not to sin. Jacob is aware of the danger. He is willing to monitor his *lips;* he lets them say only that what the Lord does is well done. He insists, however, that his *heart* has the right to "grumble against the unacceptable" and to accuse God of the "savage design" of taking his son. When Eliezer objects that Jacob is dragging "down the majesty of God against all warrant," Jacob sets him straight, drawing upon theological wisdom learned in the depths of suffering:

> Thresh not words, old man, they are but empty straw. Espouse my cause, and not God's; for He is overgreat and laugheth at thy concern, while I am but a storehouse of wailing.

For a person who embraces God the Creator and Redeemer, Jacob's demand is audacious. How could one affirm God's supreme wisdom and goodness while accusing God of being in the wrong? How could one worship God while arguing a case against God? Those who honor God shy away from complaints against God, for it seems that a god who can be justly accused ought not to be worshiped. Yet it is precisely proper piety that demands complaint when the innocent suffer. Consider Jacob's concluding words to Eliezer:

> Ah, thou God's defender, thou wilt receive thy reward and be counted high in His sight for that thou hast stood up for Him and shrewdly praised His deeds, He being God! But I tell thee He will fall upon thee! For thou wilt praise Him falsely, deceiving Him as one deceiveth a man, and wilt secretly flatter Him. Thou hypocrite, He will have none of this way of serving His cause . . . when what He has done to me shrieketh to heaven. . . . But I speak to Him otherwise, and even so am nearer to Him than thou.

Calling "right" what is manifestly wrong, just to be on God's side, is no way to speak rightly of God. Precisely because God is loving, truthful, and just, God will not put up with deceitful justifications of the unjustifiable even if it takes the form of humble piety.

From one angle, the Book of Job is all about the question of what it means to speak rightly of God in the face of innocent suffering. Did the friends who defended God speak rightly, or did Job, who wanted to take God to court? The book ends with a censure of one of Job's friends: "For you have not spoken of me what is right, as my servant Job has" (42:7).

Certainly, to argue with God, to complain against God, to hurl accusations against God is not all one ought to say about God. Jacob knew that, and said as much when he warned Eliezer that God would fall upon him for dishonesty. Jacob "grumbles" and Job wants to take God to court precisely because they believe in the ultimate triumph of God's justice in the world. To speak rightly about God in the world of innocent suffering requires argument, complaint, and accusation. Their absence would not only entail the hypocrisy of false reverence instead of true worship, as Jacob argued. It would also entail the hopelessness of merely putting up with suffering instead of seeking to overcome it.

Was I wrong to attempt to correct my friends' speech about God? The content of what I said was right, but not the timing. A "but" needed to be added to their complaints. But they needed to make their own journeys through the complaints to the God beyond God to whom they were, consciously or unconsciously, appealing and therefore whom they were in fact honoring.

I Protest, Therefore I Believe

At a dinner in honor of a prominent guest, I was seated next to a woman who works for CBS. The tsunami had just struck off the coast of Sumatra with all its destructive force, and we were talking about the magnitude of desolation, the plight of the victims, and the insanity of the event. She knew I was a theologian, so she broached the question of God. "Where was God?" she asked bluntly. "How can one believe in a good God in the face of such suffering?" And that's when I made my mistake.

The good thing is, I suppose, that the mistake was not as bad as it could have been. I could have attempted to justify God. After all, God was under attack, and I was a theologian — and a theologian who finds God immensely attractive even if sometimes totally baffling and very disturbing. But I remembered the earthquake that destroyed Lisbon in 1755 and Voltaire's *Candide*, a devastatingly witty attack on philosophical and theological optimism written partly in response. Two-thirds of Lisbon was destroyed and close to thirty thousand people died, mostly from a tidal wave and a fire that followed the earthquake. It was All Saints' Day, and "churches, with tapers burning, crumbled upon the crowds of worshipers." Brothels were mostly spared, as Voltaire was quick to note.

Ever since I read *Candide*, I have not been able to bring myself to try to defend God against the charge of impotence or lack of care with regard to horrendous evils. I certainly couldn't make it plausible to myself that "whatever is, is right" or that "partial ill is universal good." It's not so much that I've come to believe that such arguments must be wrong. Maybe I'll be persuaded by them once history has run its course and God has brought about redemption and consummation, and I am able to think with a clear head from within a world made whole. That's what Martin Luther suggested would happen in his treatise *On the Bondage of the Will.* But here and now, enmeshed as I am in a world in which suffering piles upon suffering in the course of unfolding history, I find such arguments implausible, lame, even more than a bit irritating. The good of the whole seems terribly abstract and without meaning or consolation to a human being plagued by suffering. "When death crowns the ills of suffering man, what a fine consolation to be eaten by worms!" wrote Voltaire with characteristic sarcasm.

I did not make the mistake of trying to justify God — in two minutes or less. But I did try something almost equally complex, though more plausible. I suggested to my dinner partner that the very protest against God in the face of evil in fact presupposes God's existence. Why are we disturbed about the brute and blind force of tsunamis that snuff out people's lives — including those of children who were lured, as if by some sinister design, onto the beaches by fish left exposed in the shallows because the waters had retreated just before the tidal wave came? If the world is all there is, and the world with moving tectonic plates is a world in which we happen to live, what's there to complain about? We can mourn — we've lost something terribly dear. But we can't really complain, and we certainly can't legitimately protest.

The expectation that the world should be a hospitable place, with no devastating mishaps, is tied to the belief that the world *ought* to be constituted in a certain way. And that belief — as distinct from the belief that the world just is what it is — is itself tied to the notion of a creator. And that brings us to God. It is God who makes possible our protest that there is evil in the world. And it is God against whom we protest. God is both the ground of the protest and its target. Almost paradoxically, we protest with God against God. How can I believe in God when tsunamis strike? I protest, and therefore I believe.

It was a mistake, however, to try to make this argument at that dinner. It's not that I've come to believe that the argument isn't valid. It's a fine argument, even though it leaves one with a faith that seems at odds with itself, with a God whom it is hard to abandon yet difficult to embrace. It's also not that my interlocutor was unable to follow the argument, even in such condensed form and delivered between the salad and the main course. She was smart enough for that. Yet I shouldn't have offered it, not then and there, and not as the first thing to be said about God and tsunamis.

"How can one believe in a good God in the face of such suffering?" The answer to this question depends in part on the other question my interlocutor asked me that evening, "Where was God?" My mistake was that I tried to answer the first question without answering the second. Just as God was in some mysterious way in the Crucified One, God was in the midst of the tsunami carnage, listening to every sigh, collecting every tear, resonating with the trembling of each fear-stricken heart. And just as God was in the Resurrected One, so God was in each helping hand, in each decision to sacrifice one's own life so that another could live. God suffered and God helped.

I know that, at the same time, God was also seated on God's heavenly throne. Why did the omnipotent and loving One not do something about the tsunami before it struck? I don't know. If I knew, I could justify God. But I can't. That's why I am still disturbed by the God to whom I am so immensely attracted and who won't let go of me.

The Gift of Infertility

Infertility — a gift!? Poison and a curse — that's how this unexplained infertility of ours felt to me for what seemed like an eternity. Nine years of trying to have a child of our own was like having to drink bitter waters from a poisoned well month after month. Nothing could break the sinister hold of barrenness on our lives — not strict adherence to whatever expert advice we could get, not prayer, not the latest infertility techniques, not fasting. Nothing. One hundred months' worth of hopes, all dashed against the stubborn realities of bodies that just wouldn't produce offspring. At times, like Abraham, I hoped against hope, and yet the God "who gives life to the dead and calls into existence the things that do not exist" (Rom. 4:17) wouldn't help our bodies give us an Isaac of our own.

Christian community wasn't much help, either. Every time I would go to worship, the laughter and boisterousness of the little ones milling around in the community room would remind me of unfulfilled dreams. The season of Advent was the worst. "For unto us a child is born, unto us a son is given," I would hear read or sung in hundreds of different variations. But from me a child was withheld. The miracle of Mary's conception, the rejoicing of the heavens at her newborn child, the exultation of Elizabeth all became signs of God's painful absence, not God's advent. "And the government shall be upon his shoulders...." If God's Son indeed was in charge, it seemed that he didn't care to move even his royal finger in our favor. At Christmas, I felt like the only child in a large family to whom the parents had forgotten to give gifts. Others' joy increased my sadness. "And his name shall be called wonderful, the mighty God...."

38

No, not wonderful; at best puzzling. No, not a mighty God; at best a sympathetic but disappointing divine observer.

Then came the absolutely unforgettable moment when a nurse rolled two-day-old Nathanael into the room of Lisa, his birthmother, in a maternity ward in Chino, California. She took him into her arms, held him lovingly for a moment, and then gave him to us to be our own. Several years later another birthmother, Michelle, let my wife witness the advent of our second miracle, Aaron, whom she then gave to us as our son. Nathanael was four when he cradled tiny Aaron in his arms. As I watched them, my joy as a father was complete.

It was only as I was reading the essays from the book *Hope Deferred* (Pilgrim Press), that I realized the significance of that joy. During those nine years of infertility I wasn't waiting for *a* child who stubbornly refused to come. That's what I thought at the time. In retrospect, I have come to realize that I was waiting for the two boys who now *have* come — for Nathanael and Aaron. I love them, and I want *them* in their unsubstitutable particularity, not children in general of which they happened to be exemplars. Without knowing it, I was longing for them.

Then it dawned on me: Fertility would have robbed me of my boys. From my present vantage point, that would have been a disaster — the disaster of not having what I so passionately love. Infertility was the condition for the possibility of these two indescribable gifts. And understanding that changed my attitude toward infertility. Since it gave me what I now can't imagine living without, poison was transmuted into a gift, God's strange gift. The pain of it remains, of course. But the poison is gone. Nine years of desperate trying were like one long painful childbirth, the purpose of which was to give me Nathanael and Aaron. True, had I had biological children of my own, I would have loved and wanted them, and I would have been spared the pain. But that's what *would* have happened. It didn't. I have Nathanael and Aaron. It's them that I love. It's them that I want. And it's they who redeem the arduous path that led to having them.

Infertility as a painful but welcome gift — that's my experience with reproductive loss. Others have had different experiences. I am a man, and a woman's experience might be different. Other couples struggling with infertility eventually have children who are biologically their own.

Some may decide they should not have children and proceed to live happily as a couple. Others may adopt children yet continue to long for flesh from their flesh and bone from their bone. Some may still mourn the pain of infertility or stillbirth as an irretrievable loss that no child who comes later can redeem. So I do not want to suggest that my experience is in any way exemplary. I simply share it as an invaluable redemption of my terrible loss — a redemption for which I am grateful beyond expression.

Diminished

Our hopes are a measure of our greatness. When they shrink, we ourselves are diminished. The story of American hope over the past two centuries — a story which may not be unlike the stories of hope in many other nations in our globalized world — is one of increasing narrowing — or so argues Andrew Delbanco in *The Real American Dream*. The book's three chapters are titled "God," "Nation," and "Self." The Puritans set their hopes on God and God's redemption of humanity from its incurvature upon itself — our tendency, in whatever we do, to be interested only in ourselves. In the nineteenth century, the American nation replaced God as both our hope's highest object and its surest source. Finally, the two "revolutions" toward the end of the past century — the one in the 1960s and the one in the 1980s — conspired to "install instant gratification as the hallmark of the good life." By this time the horizon of hope had shrunk to "the scale of self-pampering."

As Delbanco is well aware, the history of American hope is not as neat as his chapter titles suggest. Moreover, the stages he traces have not simply been left behind. There are many people today who do not yet worship at the altar of the self, and who still place their hopes in God or the nation. Yet Delbanco rightly observes that our culture is becoming increasingly obsessed with the self — the consuming, narcissistic self, the self incapable of extending outward in faith, love, and hope either toward God or neighbor.

When hope is "narrowed to the vanishing point of the self alone," a dark twin of hope — melancholy — ensues. What is Delbanco's balm for the wound of our melancholy? He hesitates. He wants a new faith to emerge but is uncertain of its object. Writing in the *New York Times Book Review,* Richard Rorty notes that Delbanco "is not sure whether the remedy . . . is to get religion, or instead, to resacralize the United States, replacing hope for the divine redemption with the secular hope for an ideally just America."

Rorty shows no such hesitation. Delbanco contrasts the Puritan self "expanded toward (and sometimes overwhelmed by) the vastness of God" and "a national ideal lesser than God but larger and more enduring than any individual citizen." Rorty responds:

> Why . . . should we Americans take God's word for it that he is more vast than the free, just, utopian nation of our dreams? Whitman famously called the United States of America "the greatest poem." He took narratives that featured God to be lesser poems — useful in their day, because suitable for the needs of younger humanity. But now we are more grown up. For us, the tortured adolescent writhings of Augustine, Jonathan Edwards and Graham Greene should be subjects of commiseration, not models for imitation.

Rorty recognizes that "the present culture of instant gratification makes even the Puritans look good by comparison." Yet he wants nothing like their hope. Instead, he assures us that "we have every reason to hope that once today's economic bubble bursts, once we start reinventing the interventionist state, Americans will relearn what Delbanco calls 'the lesson of Lincoln's life . . . that the quest for prosperity is no remedy for melancholy, but that a passion to secure justice by erasing the line that divides those with hope from those without hope can be.'"

"Every reason to hope"? Rorty gives us none. But leaving aside the question of whether or not his hope for a major cultural change is reasonable — it is not at all clear that even the advent of "the free, just, utopian nation of our dreams" would cure our melancholy. Imagine ourselves living in that utopian nation. If we had eyes to see beyond the bubble of our own present happiness, would not these eyes cry over injustices perpetrated by and against previous generations, injustices on which our own "free, just, utopian nation" was built? There is no justice for the living without justice for the dead, for without justice for the dead, justice for the living is an unjust justice.

Here is where God must come back into the picture even if Rorty's hope can be realized. Only the God "who gives life to the dead and calls into existence the things that do not exist" can give justice to the dead (Rom. 4:17). If you want justice, you must want more than justice here and now; if you want justice, you must want the reign of God. One reason why God is "more vast than the free, just, utopian nation of our dreams" is that without God, such a nation would remain nothing but our self-contradictory and unrealizable dream.

Early on in his book, Delbanco quotes Alexis Tocqueville:

> Men easily attain a certain equality of condition, but they can never attain as much as they desire. It perpetually retires from before them, yet without hiding itself from their sight, and in retiring draws them on. . . . They are near enough to see its charms, but too far off to enjoy them; and before they have fully tasted its delights, they die. That is the reason for the strange melancholy that haunts inhabitants of democratic countries in the midst of abundance.

Desire for worldly goods even under conditions of equality, argued Tocqueville, generates melancholy rather than cures it. Something analogous is true of justice in a world of inescapable injustice. The more you seek justice, the more you realize that it always remains outside your grasp. Hence figures such as Augustine and Edwards believed that if the world is to be enjoyed, it must be enjoyed in God, and if justice is to be realized, it must be granted to us with the gift of God's new world. Without God our hopes and we ourselves will remain diminished.

Not Optimistic

G ive yourself a treat and put Jürgen Moltmann's *Theology of Hope* under your Christmas tree. Moltmann published the book in German forty years ago. After it was translated into English three years later (1967), he became an instant theological celebrity in the United States. The book even made it to the front page of the *New York Times*. One of *Theology of Hope*'s main themes is Advent, God's coming to the world to redeem it. In the season of Advent, it may be good to remind ourselves of this extraordinarily important book.

The book's immense original popularity owes much to the fact that when it was published, "hope" was in the air. It was the "Kennedy era" in the United States and the time of the civil rights movement led by Martin Luther King, Jr. The Western world was about to experience the power of radical student movements. "Prague spring" would soon come to Czechoslovakia, a fruit of the increased democratization of socialist societies of the now defunct Second World. And in the Third World of the late 1960s, decolonization was in full swing and intellectuals toyed with Marx's ideas. *Theology of Hope* was riding a global wave of social hope. As Moltmann said, the book had its own *kairos*, or the opportune moment.

But *kairos* is an ambivalent blessing for a book. On the positive side, it propels the book to the forefront of public attention. On the negative side, it squeezes its interpretations into pre-given molds. Everybody talks about the book, but hardly anybody understands and appreciates it properly.

With some important exceptions (notably the civil rights movement), what was in the air when *Theology of Hope* came off the press ac-

44

tually was not hope but optimism. The two are easily confused. Both optimism and hope entail positive expectations with regard to the future. But, as Moltmann has argued persuasively, they are radically different stances toward reality.

Optimism is based on "extrapolative cause and effect thinking." We draw conclusions about the future on the basis of the experience with the past and present, guided by the belief that events can be explained as effects of previous causes. Since "this" has happened, we conclude that "that" is likely to happen. If an extrapolation is correct, optimism is grounded. Since my son Nathanael could pick up *Little Bear* and read it when he was in kindergarten, I could legitimately be optimistic that he would do reasonably well in the first grade. If extrapolation is incorrect, optimism is misplaced, illusory. Aaron, my two-year-old, is very good at throwing a ball. But it would be foolish for me to bet that he is likely to land a multimillion-dollar contract with a pro ball team and take care of my retirement.

Our positive expectations of the future are based mostly on such extrapolative thinking. We see the orange glow on the horizon, and we expect that morning will be bathed in sunshine. Such informed, grounded optimism is important in our private and professional lives, for the functioning of families, economy, and politics. But optimism is not hope.

One of Moltmann's lasting contributions in *Theology of Hope* was to insist that hope, unlike optimism, is independent of people's circumstances. Hope is not based on the possibilities of the situation and on correct extrapolation about the future. Hope is grounded in the faithfulness of God and therefore on the effectiveness of God's promise. And this brings me back to the theme of Advent.

Moltmann distinguished between two ways in which the future is related to us. The Latin word *futurum* expresses one way. "Future in the sense of *futurum* develops out of the past and present, inasmuch as these hold within themselves the potentiality of becoming and are 'pregnant with future.'" The Latin word *adventus* expresses the other way in which the future is related to us. Future in the sense of *adventus* is the future that comes not from the realm of what is or what was, but from the realm of what is not yet, "from outside," from God.

45

Optimism is based on the possibilities of things as they have come to be; hope is based on the possibilities of God irrespective of how things are. Hope can spring up even in the valley of the shadow of death; indeed, it is there that it becomes truly manifest. The figure of hope in the New Testament is Abraham, who hoped against all hope because he believed in the God "who gives life to the dead and calls into existence the things that do not exist" (Rom. 4:17-18). Hope thrives even in situations which, for extrapolative cause-and-effect thinking, can elicit only utter hopelessness. Why? Because hope is based on God's coming into the darkness to dispel it with divine light.

Every year in the Advent season we read the prophet Isaiah: "The people who walked in darkness have seen a great light; those who lived in a land of deep darkness — on them light has shined" (Isa. 9:2). This is what Christmas is all about — something radically new that cannot be generated out of the conditions of this world. It does not emerge. It comes. We do not extrapolate it. God promises it.

If darkness has descended upon you and your world, you need not try to persuade yourself that things are not as bad as they seem or to search desperately for reasons to be optimistic. Remind yourself instead of a very simple fact: the light of the One who was in the beginning with God shines in the darkness, and the darkness has not overcome it. If you need a lengthy and plausible argument to support this invitation, unwrap that Moltmann book from under your Christmas tree, get yourself a warm drink, and enter the world of Advent, of promise, of hope.

Narratives of Hope

"**A**merica once again considers itself the capital of the future," wrote Ronald Brownstein in 1998, commenting on "the return of American optimism." "Return" may not be quite the right word: even in its more pessimistic moods, mainstream America exudes a kind of optimism rarely found elsewhere in the world. Which makes talk about the "return of optimism in America" even more significant. By all standards, this is optimism *extraordinaire*.

At the end of the century, pessimistic *fin-de-siecle* moods seem in retreat before a "pitiless procession of good news. The economy, now in its sixth year of growth, has driven down unemployment to its lowest level in a quarter century. The federal budget deficit, which once threatened to submerge Washington, is evaporating like a puddle on a sunny day. Crime is way down, and the rates of divorce and out-of-wedlock birth are stabilizing after years of explosive growth."

The consequence? Bright-eyed Americans, buoyed by a heightened sense of security, are smiling at the dawn of a new millennium. The "city on the hill" of past centuries has become the "capital of the future" — a vision not too far removed from Ebenezer Baldwin's musings in 1776 that America would be "the principal seat of that glorious kingdom, which Christ shall erect upon the earth in the latter days."

Observing the capital from the periphery, one gets a sense that something has gone wrong — the same sense one gets when reading

This essay, originally published in *Christian Century* 115/3 (1998), was co-authored by Miroslav Volf and Tammy Williams.

about American teenagers with unexceptional academic skills who nonetheless extol the superiority of their mathematical performance as compared to that of their peers in other countries. The problem is not that they feel good about themselves even though their performance is shabby; the problem is that they need to believe that they in fact perform better than others in order to feel good about themselves.

The mainstream culture seems to reason: If you keep pumping personal and national egos, the world will be all right. Don't worry about actual math scores or the many lamentable public schools. Don't worry about the "dead streets" of inner cities, about low wages for unskilled laborers, about racism that still raises its ugly head. Instead, indulge in dreams about "the capital of the future." For when Americans feel good, they have babies, they work, they achieve.

But will the "feel-good" strategy work? And if it does, at what price?

The controversial film *Amistad,* which chronicles an 1839 slave mutiny, casts a brief shadow over the dawn of the new millennium by relating a messy story that threatens our sense of optimism, even superiority. We need precisely this kind of complex narrative that compels us to confront the underside of our history and thereby helps us imagine a just and peaceful future.

Named after the Spanish slave ship that was commandeered by its African captives off the coast of Cuba, *Amistad* portrays the capture and imprisonment of rebel slaves by American authorities and their subsequent grant of freedom after their legal claims reached the United States Supreme Court. The story of the "triumph of liberty" is told against the backdrop of the harrowing saga of the Middle Passage and its "rites of initiation" — the stages of captured African, overcrowded cargo, brutalized slave, and finally profitable property in the New World.

Those who would walk away from the riveting court scenes concluding that "the system really does work" can do so only after seeing unbridled corruption at the highest levels in the political and judicial system. Whatever the film's historical or cinematic shortcomings, by asking both slave and abolitionist, "What is your story?" *Amistad* underscores that we can dream of the future rightly only if we do not suppress the horrors of the present and the past.

Listening to voices from the underside of the past or of the present is not without its dangers, however. "Guilt-tripping," "invoking bad feelings," and "not getting the story right to begin with" are the hazards of such an exercise, and *Amistad* has not entirely escaped them, according to some critics.

But there is a greater danger than that of conjuring up uncomfortable memories or not getting them quite right, namely, that after suppressing or ignoring the stories that make us uneasy we will embrace myths that tell us only what we like to hear. We justify the unjustifiable, we reconcile ourselves with the unreconcilable; we project our own evil onto others and punish them for our sins; we say "all is well" — we even believe that "all is well" when ruin is about to take place. Simple, custom-made myths, whispered into our ears by the evil spirit appearing as an angel of light, pose a more serious threat to our well-being than the messy, unedited narratives.

What we need at the threshold of a new millennium are not stories of optimism but narratives of hope. On a psychological level, optimism is about "feeling good" about yourself because you are "the capital of the future." The obverse of such optimism is the denial of the horrors of history and disregard for ruined lives. Authentic Christian hope, on the other hand, is about the promise that the wrongs of the past can be set aright and that the future need not be a mere repetition of the past.

To hope does not mean to dream ourselves into a different reality, but to embrace the promise that this reality, suffused with suffering, will be transformed into God's new world. We must acknowledge the underside of our history; otherwise, we will never be redeemed. The good news is that those who hope can acknowledge the dark side of their history because the divine promise frees them from captivity to the past.

FAMILY MATTERS

Married Love

D early beloved,
    Recent surveys report that adults in their twenties have high hopes for themselves and marriage, but a low appraisal of marriage in general.

You have high hopes for yourselves. You have found in each other a soulmate, a person with whom to share the joys and sorrows of life and practice the art of love. But the institution of marriage is in crisis. Your peers have deep reservations about "happily ever after." One in two marriages end up in divorce, while those partners who stay together often end up "sleeping with the enemy." You are about to embark upon a most wonderful journey, yet dangers lurk.

For some people, the crisis of marriage is a crisis of authority. They respond by bolstering the rule of the husband. The man should command; the woman should obey. If he is above and she below, order and stability will reign. But this is a questionable strategy. Unless the man is a saint — and no man is — the woman will either be oppressed or seek surreptitiously to subvert the husband's rule and exercise dominion.

Others seek to avert a crisis by stressing equality — one partner, one vote. The wife should not submit to the husband, but each to the other. It is hard to dispute that, on the whole, equality is better than inequality, common agreement better than autocratic decisions, mutual submission better than the rule of the one over the other. But will the stress on equality steer your marriage out of crisis? It will help. Yet egalitarianism in and of itself will not make a marriage thrive. Each partner can be equal, each free, and still thinking only about himself or herself. Marriage partners are then like business partners. They make contracts with one another, and they will break them to pursue new partnerships if better returns seem likely.

A good marriage is not a contract, but a covenant. Contracts are conditional: we are obliged to keep the terms only if our partners are doing the same. Covenants, however, are unconditional. We are obliged even if the partners break the terms. Contracts are temporary: we are bound by them only as long as it suits us (provided we pay the consequences of breaking them). Covenants are durable: we are bound by the marriage covenant "until death do us part." Contracts are governed by the pursuit of one's interests. Covenants are governed by the demands of love.

Love between partners is a sparkle in the eye, a warm feeling, a throbbing desire of the flesh and the soul. Erotic love is God's wonderful gift, and I hope that you won't let its flame die out. But love is more than *eros.* It has to do with how you treat each other when dishes need to be washed or garbage taken out, when misunderstandings arise and when one has transgressed against the other. Love is not just the desire to be united with the other, but action on behalf of the other, and constancy in pursuit of his or her well-being. Such love "makes all things equal," as the ancients knew. But such love entails more than just the practice of equality.

Here is one way to put it. Soon you will want to purchase a home. If you are lucky, you'll get a good deal — you'll pay less than the house is worth. If you are unlucky, you'll get a raw deal and discover that you paid more than you should have. If you are equitable, you'll hope for a fair deal and your contract will oblige you to pay what the house is actually worth.

But with love it is different. To give less than you expect to receive is selfishness, no matter how warm your heart feels in the other's presence. To give as much as you receive is to be fair. But to love is to give more than you hope to receive. Is love a raw deal? From the perspective of contractual relations it is. But love has its own rewards. Remember that Jesus said it is more blessed to give than to receive. The return that I get when I practice self-giving love is not more to me, but more to us — more to the beauty of our common love.

This kind of love will be most difficult after you have injured each other. At this joyous hour, you may find the thought of injury negative, even morbid. Yet if the joy of this moment is to be a celebration of love and not just of some fuzzy feeling, you need to anticipate injuries and think about what will be needed to heal them.

In an old Jewish story about creation, God decided to create the world, then foresaw all the sin that human beings would commit against God and each other. The only way God could continue was to decide to forgive the world before creating it. Strange as it may seem, the commitment to forgive comes before creation. Similarly, commitment to forgive comes before marriage vows.

I know that you will not rely on the rule of the one over the other. But I hope that you'll do more than insist on equal rights. Commit yourself to the adventure of a love that seeks to give more than it expects to receive. Then the miracle of a lasting and fulfilled marriage will be yours.

Ambiguity and Grace

I had just settled into my hotel room. Behind me was a five-hour drive to Mammoth and a good four hours of skiing (including the double black diamond run "Wipeout," where I helped a lone skier — who turned out to be a near compatriot, a Slovene — retrieve his equipment after he had slid some one hundred fifty yards down the slope unharmed). After having a beer with him and relaxing in the spa for a while, I went to my room and called home to give my wife my telephone number at the hotel. I had barely said "Hi" when she exclaimed, exuberant as I had never heard her before, "Guess what!"

I guessed it in the split second she left me to do the guessing. "We are parents!" she burst out before I could say anything. A nine-year-old dream already grown rather tired and unsure how much longer it wanted to live had suddenly come true. I was elated.

I wanted to know everything but was too excited to sit in a hotel room miles away in order to hear it all. So I got the basics — it was a boy, he was healthy, his birth mom was doing well — and hopped into the car (though not without managing first to lock myself out of the hotel room, with all my luggage inside!). During the four-hour drive back — yes, it took four hours, not five! — a smile stuck to my face and my mind revisited the events that preceded the good news.

The day before, and, as it turned out, only four hours before our son was born, a social worker had visited our home to complete the home study. For the second time we were asked the same difficult questions. What kind of baby were we willing to adopt? What racial mixture? (How about one-quarter Hispanic, one-eighth Asian, one-eighth African-

American, one-quarter Caucasian, and one-quarter Middle Eastern?) What health conditions? (Club foot — severe, medium, light, none?) What about the birth mother and her practices before and during pregnancy? (Light use of drugs before she knew she was pregnant and moderate smoking during pregnancy?) Two hours of deliberating about such questions drained me emotionally.

I knew why we were being asked the questions, and I was glad that we had a choice. Yet I felt deep unease even entertaining them. After all, I was not shopping for a car or getting a dog, but seeking to adopt a human being. Had I been a birth father, I would have embraced any child born to me — at least I hope so. As an adoptive father, I could exclude the child I did not want or did not think I could adequately care for. It seemed that I had the right to do so without feeling guilty, and yet I felt an obligation to embrace the first child offered us.

As I was coming to terms with the idea of my own future child's being an object of my discriminating choice, I was faced with the equally ambiguous notion that I as a parent was an object of discriminating choice. First we were screened by the adoption agency. Our family histories were recorded, our practices and values taken note of, our home examined. Are we worthy to be parents? seemed the bottom line. Had I been a birth father, no one would have asked the question; the sheer fact of my existence would have justified me as a father. Now I had to earn what would have otherwise come as a gift. I resisted the requirement to earn the right to parenthood — maybe, as a friend who adopted suggested, because deep down I felt that one could never be deserving of a child.

After the screening by the agency came something much worse: the birthmother's choice. The policy of the adoption agency with which we were working was to show a number of profiles of adoptive parents to a birthmother and let her choose the couple to whom she wanted to entrust her child. She would examine the write-up on us by the social worker, see our pictures, read our letters to the birthmother, and then choose. "Well, Mr. Volf, I do not like your forty-one years of age, and your bald head does not sit well with me. Next file, please!"

Just as I thought there was something amiss with my deciding whether or not I wanted a particular child, so I also thought it was not quite right that my fatherhood would rest on someone's judgment about my suitability and desirability. And yet, just as it was good that I had the choice about the child, so it was good that adoption agencies were screening people and that birthmothers could decide with whom to place their child.

Though I was so excited on our way to the hospital that I turned the wrong way on a one-way street with a police car only a few yards away, I nevertheless carried with me this profound moral ambiguity surrounding the adoption. And then I saw him — fine-featured little head with wide-open eyes, protruding out of a "burrito wrap." That very instant I knew that I had received a most incredible gift. Its radiance shone brightly through all the ambiguities of the adoption process. What seemed like the placement of an order — "I do not want this, but would be open to that" — was in fact experienced fully as a gift. And what felt like a demand to earn a right — "You must do this and be that" — was in fact experienced unequivocally as grace.

People sometimes ask me what theological insights I have learned as a father. This is one of them: Divine grace comes often to us through the ambiguities of life, not apart from them.

She Who Truly Loves

T he first thing I saw was a tear — an unforgettable giant tear in the
big brown eye of a ten-year-old girl. Then I saw tears in her mother's
eyes. In these tears, just enough joy was mixed with pain to underscore
the pain's severity: joy at seeing him, their three-month-old brother and
son, and intense pain at having kissed him good-bye when he was just
two days old; the ache that he, flesh of their flesh, was being brought to
them for a brief visit by two strangers who are now his parents; the affliction of knowing that the joy of loving him as a mother and sister usually
do will never be theirs.

The joy and the pain of those tears led me to a repentance of sorts.
My image of mothers who place their children for adoption was not as
bad as my image of the fathers involved, but it was not entirely positive
either. I could not shake the feeling that there was something deficient in
the act. The taint of "abandonment" marred it, an abandonment that
was understandable, possibly even inescapable and certainly tragic, but
abandonment nonetheless. To give one's child to another is to fail in the
most proper duty of a parent: to love no matter what.

Somewhere in my mind, a famous verse from Isaiah colored the way
I was reading birthmothers' actions: "Can a woman forget her nursing
child, or show no compassion for the child of her womb? Even these may
forget, yet I will not forget you" (Isa. 49:15). A good mother, I thought,
ought to be like Israel's God, unable to "give up" her child (cf. Hos. 11:8).

But a mother is not God, only a fragile human being living in a tragic
world. So why think immediately of abandonment because she decides
to place her child for adoption? The tears of our son's birthmother and

59

the actions which, like a beautiful plant, were watered by those tears, suggested that my view of at least some birthmothers may be not only mistaken but also deeply flawed. I needed to repent and alter the image.

Later, as I was reflecting on those tears, I came across a passage in Aristotle's *Nicomachean Ethics.* "Witness the pleasure that mothers take in loving their children. Some mothers put their infants out to nurse, and though knowing and loving them do not ask to be loved by them in return, if it be impossible to have this as well, but are content if they see them prospering; they retain their own love for them even though the children, not knowing them, cannot render them any part of what is due to a mother." The text comes from Aristotle's discussion of friendship. He employs the example to make plausible that "in its essence friendship seems to consist more in giving than receiving affection." For Aristotle, a birthmother manifests the kind of love characteristic of a true friend, a love exercised for that friend's sake, not for benefits gained from the relationship.

"It is hard to know that you have a child in the world, far away from you," wrote our son's birthmother in her first letter to us. It is hard because love passionately desires the presence of the beloved. And yet it was that same love that took deliberate and carefully studied steps that would lead to his absence. In a letter she wrote for him to read when he grows up, she tells him that her decision to place him for adoption was made for his own good. "I did it for you," she wrote repeatedly and added, "Some day you will understand."

She loved him for his own sake, and therefore would rather suffer his absence if he flourished than enjoy his presence if he languished; her sorrow over his avoidable languishing would overshadow her delight in his presence. For a lover, it is more blessed to give than to receive, even when giving pierces the lover's heart. My image of birthmothers had changed: "she who does not care quite enough" has become "she who truly loves."

When we parted after our first post-adoption meeting, a smile had replaced the tears on the face of our son's birthmother. Now it was my turn to cry. Back at home, with him in one arm and an open album she made for him in the other, I shed tears over the tragedy of her love. Despite an intense affection for our son — no, because of such affection — I thought there was something profoundly wrong about his being with us and not with her. In a good world, in a world in which the best things are not sometimes so terribly painful, he and she would delight and thrive in each other's love.

The encounter with our son's birthmother left an indelible mark not so much on my memory as on my character. She helped me articulate what it means to be a good parent. A vision of parenting that was buried under many impressions and opinions emerged clearly on the horizon of my consciousness. I ought to love him the way she loved him, for his own sake, not for mine. I must not pervert my love into possession. I can hold onto him only if I let go of him.

But how can I let go of him whom I long so intensely to hold? The only way I know is by placing him in the arms of the same God from whom we received him. I remembered another deeply pained woman — a woman who suffered not so much because she had to give away her child but because, like my wife and me, she needed a miracle to receive a child. It was Hannah, the mother of Samuel. She was given the child she so desperately desired because she was willing to let go of him (1 Sam. 1:11). Even those of us who will not set our children "before God as Nazirites," as Hannah did, will love them best if we hold them — in God's arms.

Negative Externality

"**W**hy shouldn't parents be treated as badly as smokers?" asked the writer rhetorically. After all, "children, just like cigarettes or mobile phones, clearly impose a negative externality on people who are near them." The shooting of innocents at Columbine High reminded me again of these comments, which appeared in an editorial in the *Economist*. At first I thought that it was written tongue in cheek by a person who had just suffered through a nine-hour flight with a screaming baby in the next seat. But halfway through the article I stopped smiling.

"Smoking, driving and mobile phones all cause what economists call 'negative externalities,'" states the editorial. "That is, the costs of these activities to other people tend to exceed the costs to the individuals of their proclivities. The invisible hand of the market fumbles, leading resources astray. Thus, because a driver's private motoring costs do not reflect the costs he imposes on others in the form of pollution and congestion, he uses the car more than is socially desirable. Likewise, it is argued, smokers take too little care to ensure that their acrid fumes do not damage other people around them." Along with smoking, driving, and mobile phones, children are "objects" which tend to impose high negative externalities on others.

The *Economist* applied the argument to air travel and complained that "parents do not bear the full costs." The proposed solution? Create "child-free zones" and charge children more than adults. The argument begs to be extended to eating in restaurants, frequenting parks and beaches, using streets, indeed to playing in one's own backyard (at least in homes on lots smaller than six acres). Imagine the world as one large airplane on which we all ride from birth to death. The logic of the proposal would have us create large child-free zones and tax parents until their children reach adulthood. It's even worse. Arguably, children are ultimately the "beneficiaries" of their own lives. So the logic of the proposal may even nudge us to ensure that parents are properly reimbursed for the expense and remunerated for negative externalities they have suffered from their own children — provided the children don't object to having been sent into the world.

Behind the proposal lies an elemental forgetfulness so typical of the liberal tradition. It seems to have escaped the editorial writer that, as Jeremy Bentham noted critically of John Locke, human beings do not come into the world as grown-ups. If you complain that children impose negative externalities on you, don't forget the negative externalities you yourself imposed on others. If you want to put a price-tag on the nuisance of having children around, then pay the debts you yourself have incurred. Why should parents not be treated as badly as smokers? Justice demands it. We have all accumulated debts in childhood.

Right around the time I read the *Economist* editorial, my wife was working on an article on children in the Gospels. Here are a few central sentences from her text. On Mark 9:33-37 she wrote: "Love for the least is the way to the new greatness that should characterize Jesus' disciples. . . . Rather than suffering neglect on account of their presumed insignificance, they are to be put in the very center of the community's life and ministry."

Mark 10:13-16 elicited this comment: "Far from being disqualified . . . little children epitomize how to enter the reign of God. They are model participants and recipients. . . . Adult believers are to understand their own identity and attainments as irrelevant to participation in the reign of God."

Matthew 18:1-5 suggests, she argued, that "high status (being the greatest) is gained through childlikeness . . . , and childlikeness is described as humbleness." The pinnacle of Mark 9:33-37, she maintained, is the claim that "the welcoming of a little child in Jesus' name is a test of one's openness to Jesus himself. For the little child functions as Jesus himself and God who sent him."

She summed up Jesus' treatment of children by noting a radical challenge that it presents for the adult world: "The Gospels thus teach not merely how to make an adult world kinder and more just for children. The Gospels teach the arrival of the small world, the little child's world. They cast judgment on the adult world as such because it is not the child's world."

Justice demands that we not equate parents with smokers and children's noise with "acrid fumes." But more than justice is at stake here. As Jesus' comments about children and adults' relation to them imply, at stake is nothing less than the character of our social world. The *Economist* presupposes a world in which the one who is least dependent and can acquire the most is the greatest. Jesus' ministry, of which the treatment of children is a paradigmatic case, presupposes that persons belong to a community of grace in which others' fragility and even "rowdiness" are opportunities of service; the greatest is the one who humbles him or herself and serves the little ones.

Those who know a bit about me might object: "A father of a one-year-old is protesting here." My response is, "No, a parent of a future teenager is protesting here." There is nothing more important we can do to stem violence in our schools and our culture that provided an environment in which the Columbine shooting could happen than to take Jesus seriously — to refuse to treat children as "negative externalities" and to work for the arrival of God's "small world."

But I Am Not Abraham

For some time now I have been both attracted to and troubled by the story of Abraham's journey to present his son Isaac as a burnt offering in the land of Moriah. I was moved by Abraham's extraordinary devotion to God but repelled by the thought that it made him willing to sacrifice his only child. So I turned with considerable interest to an article in a recent issue of the *International Journal of Systematic Theology*. In discussing Kierkegaard's reading of the story, Murray Rea argues there that "while no justification of Abraham's action . . . may be offered, he is nevertheless to be admired for trusting in God beyond the limits of his understanding." Such trust is admirable, however, Rea went on to say, "only in the context of a long life of obedience and love."

I was reading the text and silently nodding to myself in agreement. When I turned to the last page, I saw a drawing of a small hand. A few days earlier I had been "reading" the journal with my son Nathanael, then twenty months old. Bored because there were no pictures of people or animals, he decided to help the editors out and add some spice to the journal. "Daddy, ruka [which means 'hand' in Croatian]," he said while placing his hand on the white portion of the page at the end of the article. I took a pencil and sketched the outline of his tiny fingers.

"Would you have done it?" asked, in my imagination, a twelve-year-old Nathanael — a boy about the age when Isaac could have carried the wood for the sacrifice.

"No, son," I quickly responded, shuddering at the very thought of it. "I would never have done it."

"But weren't you agreeing with Mr. Rea?"

"Yes, but I am not Abraham."

"And what if God told you to 'offer your only son, Nathanael, whom you love'? Wouldn't you obey God?"

"It is not so easy to recognize God's voice. Do you remember the story of Samuel? He thought his old master was calling him, when in fact God was speaking to him. Mostly it happens the other way around."

"Yes, but Samuel was then only a boy."

"If I heard a voice telling me to offer you as a burnt offering, I wouldn't believe it was God's. I can't help but think that Kant was partly right."

"Kant?"

"Yes, Immanuel Kant, the famous philosopher. He thought Abraham should have responded to the voice by saying, 'It is quite certain that I ought not to kill my innocent son, but I am not certain and I cannot ever become certain that you, the "you" who is appearing to me, are God.'"

"Kant thought that Abraham was wrong, but you think Abraham was right?"

"Yes, Kant was wrong about *Abraham*. Not all journeys into the realm beyond ethics are forbidden. But Kant would have been right, had he been talking about almost anyone else. Compared to Abraham, I am spiritually like Samuel, a little boy who does not know."

"Oh, come on, Dad! You are a big man and you teach theology at Yale!"

"No, Nathanael, Abraham was among the greatest of the great. God tells him to leave the land of his parents — don't you get any ideas! He obeys, and it turns out to have been the right thing to do. God tells him that he will have a son, even though physically he and Sarah could not have children, and Isaac is born. Abraham knew how to hear God. See, his ability to recognize God's voice and his willingness to trust God reinforced each other."

"You mean that when Abraham told Isaac that 'God will provide the lamb,' he was not pulling the wool over his eyes?"

"I don't think he was. Abraham knew two things: he knew that God spoke to him and he knew that he could trust God."

"Did Abraham then obey while knowing all along that he would not have to do what God commands?"

"'Knowing' is too strong. 'Trusting' is better."

"But he almost killed Isaac!"

"Almost."

"That's good. Isaac wasn't killed. Thank goodness the story has nothing to do with you and me. It's about a great man, a father we should admire but not imitate."

"That's right, we should not imitate Abraham in this respect. The Old Testament specifically forbids child sacrifice. Still, the story has something to do with you and me. Suppose," I continued, "that God asked me, 'Who is more important to you, Nathanael or I?' What do you think I should say?"

"You should say 'God'!"

"Why?"

"You told me that my name means 'God has given,' right?"

"Right."

"Well, if it were not for the giver, there would be no gift."

"Smart boy! To receive you as a gift from God rightly, I must love God more than you. In a sense, that's what Abraham did. Are you jealous?"

"No. If it were not for God, you would not have me and I would not have you; we would not be playing soccer and skiing together, and you would not be teaching me to drive even though I am only twelve, and you. . . ."

My thought was interrupted by the sound of little feet running toward me. Oblivious to the grave conversation I was having in my mind with his older self, my little son buffed his head in my lap and demanded, "Tickle!" I did, half regretting that I could not go on to tell his older self about the God who, far from requiring us to sacrifice our children, sacrificed himself in the person of his Son for our salvation. Then he'd probably ask me about divine child abuse and I'd tell him something about the mysteries of the Trinity. Another time.

Will My Son Be a Christian?

The statistics are clearly in my favor. An overwhelming majority of children adopt the religion of their parents. So I shouldn't worry. It is highly probable that my son Nathanael — and his younger brother, Aaron — will grow up in some sense a Christian. But I still worry, mainly because I am not satisfied with his being a Christian "in some sense." Mindful of Kierkegaard's critique of Christendom, I'd almost rather that he be no Christian than an indifferent Christian, or, even worse, a zealous Christian manipulating faith to promote his own selfish ends. But I want him to embrace Christianity as a faith by which to live and for which to die.

But how do I pass on that kind of faith? The question is gnawing at me daily, though it bites the strongest during the high seasons of the church calendar such as Advent and Lent, when we concentrate on the mysteries that lie at the heart of our faith — God's coming into the world and the Lamb's taking away the sins of the world.

A few months ago I was leafing through Joseph Yerushalmi's classic book on Jewish history and memory, *Zakhor,* and came across a letter that Franz Kafka wrote to his father. I underlined the following text twice:

> You really had brought some traces of Judaism with you from the ghetto-like village community. It was not much and it dwindled a little more in the city and during your military service; but still, the impressions and memories of your youth did just about suffice for some sort of Jewish life.... Even in this there was still Judaism enough, but it was

too little to be handed on to the child; it all dribbled away while you were passing it on.

What will Nathanael and Aaron see in my hands as I am trying to transmit to them the Christian faith? Just traces of what has slipped between my fingers, partly because there was not much in my hands to begin with? I'd be devastated if this were to happen.

Clearly, you cannot pass on what has dribbled away. But when it comes to faith, the trouble is that you may not be able to pass on even what you firmly hold in your hands. Take my father. The child of a Catholic father and a Baptist mother, my father drifted away from faith by the time he was in his early teens. He returned to it in the concentration camp. No, it was not the horror of hovering for months between life and death that did the trick. To the contrary. Immense suffering intensified his rebellion against God. He was in hell right now, my father thought, so nothing worse could happen to him later. As for a God who would let such suffering befall human beings, if he existed he deserved to be cursed and spat upon.

But then my father encountered a man who was rebelling against the horror around him in a different way. Raging hunger, hard labor, and thousands of daily humiliations neither extinguished the sparkle in his eyes nor made his hands weary of helping others. Gradually, my father started believing this strange man who dared to talk about God's power and love in the midst of hell. Miracle of miracles, no sooner had my father embraced the Christian faith than he was appointed a baker for the whole camp — by communist guards who were out to destroy all religion! His hunger was gone, and he was his own boss who could appoint the evangelizer as his helper.

From his conversion until his dying day, my father's faith was genuine, deep, and intense. None of it dribbled away as he was passing it on to me. Yet what did I do with his gift? Sandwiched between the trials of being a preacher's kid in a church in which everybody knew everybody else, and being a laughingstock at an officially atheist school, I decided that I wanted nothing to do with religion. God was just plain too much trouble — intellectually and practically.

My problem was not my father's empty hands. It was rather that what I found in them was impossible to bear. His faith demanded too much and was at odds with the prevailing cultural sensibilities. So I rejected it. When I was brought back to faith it was through the prayers of my devout mother. Every evening when her prodigal son would go out, she would wait on her knees for him to return. It was not enough for me to be handed a robust faith; I had to be made to *want* a faith that, in Bonhoeffer's famous words, "bids a man to come and die."

Nathanael was barely two and unable to form proper sentences when he asked the biggest of all questions. "Daddy, what God mean?" I was taken aback, but then began talking about the One who created the skies, the oceans, and the dry land; the birds, the fish and all the other animals. I sensed that I was talking past him and felt humiliated as a theologian (though I am not sure that one could answer this question in any way that a two-year-old would understand). I told an acquaintance about my predicament. She responded, "It is not what you say that matters, but what you do." "And that is supposed to be helpful?" I thought to myself. She increased the burden of my responsibility, but I was not sure how much it would help Nathanael.

Then I remembered my mother's prayers. Right language about God matters; godly life matters even more. Yet neither will suffice. If the seed sown by word and deed is to grow and bear fruit, it will need the life-giving water of God's Spirit. So I abandoned trust either in statistics about religious belonging or in the genuineness and strength of my own faith. I vowed to pray.

On Jordan's Banks

I never used to be much of a pilgrim. Since ancient times, such travelers have journeyed to sites of religious significance in order to deepen their faith. But I was raised a Pentecostal, and in one regard our brand of faith was very modern: unlike virtually all pre-modern people, we did not recognize any "sacred places." For us, all places were alike to God, because God had created them all. All places were "sacred" to humanity, because God could be experienced anywhere.

I was forty-five when I first visited Jerusalem, the Holy City, where centuries of history vital to our faith occurred, culminating in our Lord's crucifixion and resurrection. The "Holy City" was a huge disappointment. The "holy sites" struck me as inauthentic in two ways. First, it seemed dubious that any of the events in Jesus' life had actually happened at those sites. Little historical evidence existed, and only pious legend linked the sites directly to Jesus. Second, and equally important, the sites themselves offered little help for growth in holiness. How is one to benefit spiritually from a visit to the church of the Holy Sepulcher, when it is divided up and run by a quarrelsome group of monks, the embodiment of the exact opposite of the message of reconciliation conveyed by the cross? Or what is one to make of the ubiquitous merchant stands, with their gaudy little religious objects? By "marketing" him, they seemed to mock the very Jesus Christ with whom the pilgrims were looking for a deeper encounter. For did he not cleanse the Temple because merchants had turned the house of God into a "den of robbers"?

When my oldest son, Nathanael, and I decided to take a father-son trip to the Hashemite Kingdom of Jordan, one of the first stops on our itinerary — on the way to the pleasures of floating in the Dead Sea — was a visit to the Baptism Site. Why did I, a reluctant and skeptical pilgrim, take him to a holy site and on a pilgrimage? The Baptism Site, the historic location where Jesus reportedly was baptized and began his ministry, is different.

For one, the scriptural, archeological, and documentary evidence to support the historical authenticity of this particular site was quite strong. The Gospel of John states explicitly that John was baptizing on the eastern bank of the river Jordan, at "Bethany across the Jordan" (John 1:28; see also 10:40). In 1996, archeological discoveries helped locate with relative certainty where John the Baptist lived and where he was baptizing. On the eastern bank of the Jordan River, they found the ruins of the ancient church (c. A.D. 500) dedicated to John the Baptist, as well as the remains of two basilicas linked through marble steps to a cruciform baptistery designed for baptisms in the flowing water. Further support was provided by the writings of an early pilgrim (A.D. 333): "Five miles from the Dead Sea in the Jordan is the place where the Lord was baptized by John, and above the far bank at the same place is the hillock from which Elijah was taken up to heaven." Sure enough, a mile or so away is Elijah's Hill, another archeological site where remains of an ancient monastery and churches were discovered on the hill at which Elijah is reported to have been taken up into heaven by a whirlwind in a chariot of fire. In the vicinity is Wadi al-Kharrar, believed to be Kerith Ravine, where God commanded Elijah to seek refuge from King Ahab and Queen Jezebel. And all of this is on the historic Christian pilgrimage route connecting Jerusalem and Mt. Nebo, the mountain from which Moses surveyed the Promised Land before he died.

To my surprise, I was completely taken by the Baptism Site. Aside from the likely historical authenticity of the place, I was struck forcibly by its "spiritual authenticity." There we were, at the foot of Elijah's Hill, and all we could see in this austere desert place were the archeological remains of a monastery, a church, a prayer hall. My mind was drawn to the two great prophets of the Old and New Testaments, Elijah and John, and their struggles against Ahab and Jezebel, Herod and Herodias. We took a slow stroll down the pedestrian trail meandering through the ancient trees of Wadi al-Kharrar toward the remains of the Church of John the Baptist, and then further down to the Jordan River, and we sensed that we were in a different world. We were deeply moved by the knowledge that there, near the shores of the Dead Sea — the lowest point on the surface of the earth — began the ministry of the One who was to reunite heaven and earth.

The modern Baptism Site is relatively new as a place of pilgrimage. You'll find construction going on. New churches, a monastery, and a pilgrimage house are being built on the grounds — provided free of charge by the Jordanian government — including the two Roman Catholic churches whose cornerstone Pope Benedict XVI blessed during his recent visit. But wisely, these structures are placed at a distance from the "holy sites"; they are there to aid pilgrims as they seek spiritual refreshment in connection with the sites themselves, not to insinuate themselves in place of the sites. Moreover, until now the Royal Commission of the Baptismal Site has resisted what must be immense pressure to turn the Baptism Site into a marketplace for religious memorabilia. You can still purchase souvenirs, but only at the visitors' center, not at the sites themselves.

A few hundred yards away from Elijah's Hill, at the edge of Wadi al-Kharrar, two small caves were discovered. They were dug into the upper layers of the Lisan marl cliffs as dwellings for hermit monks, equipped with prayer niches carved into their eastern walls. If you stand at the mouth of the cave, you see the Baptism Site and, across the Jordan River, Jericho. On a clear day, I was told, you can even see Jerusalem in the distance. Here, anchored to sacred places and nourished by sacred memories of Christ's life and sacred hopes of his coming, hermits sought to draw closer to God by weaving their own lives into the larger narrative of God's dealings with humanity. In a very small measure, this is what the Baptism Site made possible for my son and me. As Nathanael wrote with rich simplicity in his journal that evening: "I felt somehow connected with Jesus."

Remember That You Will Die

A metal door opened, and we were invited in. Draped sloppily in white linen was a body on a table, frozen and immovable. I immediately recognized the feet, and then, after taking a step, I saw the beloved face. I bent over and gave the cold forehead one final kiss. A wind of deep sadness shook my whole body and my eyes welled up with tears. I had just arrived in Osijek, Croatia, where my father had died three days earlier. I wanted to see him and touch him one last time. Him? "He is not here," I said to my sister after I had composed myself. "This is only his body."

Back in the United States, the news of his departure had left me numb. My mind oscillated between a deep sense of sorrow and the inability to believe the indubitable. Once I saw and touched his dead body, I was able to let loose a bit of the present drenched in mourning and make excursions into the past, his and mine. In this life, death has robbed the two of us of our common present and future. What remained was our past. Now that I could no longer escape it, his death began to gather together his life for me, and from the most striking memories a portrait emerged. I was a bit surprised at what I saw.

I was aware, of course, that life looks different from the perspective of its end than from any of the points along the way. As a spiritual exercise, I would occasionally try to elevate myself imaginatively from the present and see my life from the vantage point of its end. A few years ago, when I was on a sabbatical in Tübingen, Germany, I would walk through a graveyard on my way to and from my office. As I entered the gate, I would pass the tomb of the Goes family. The letters were written in capitals, and I could not help but read the text in English: "MARIANNE GOES, HEINRICH GOES, OTTO GOES," and then I would add, "And eventually we all go!"

At the other gate, on my way out of the graveyard, I would pass by the tomb of the famous Tübingen theologian of the last century, Ferdinand Christian Baur. During the minute that it took me to walk between the two graves, I would place my work as a theologian in the light of my own imagined end; I wanted to make sure that I was not seduced by day-to-day pressures or contemporary concerns to betray what truly mattered. This was my own way of extending to myself the old greeting of the Trappist monks: "Remember that you will die!"

My father was a man of few words. For him, talk was cheap and bothersome; deeds mattered. I expected that I would remember him by his accomplishments. After all, he was a successful man. In addition to being a well-respected pastor for over thirty years and a prominent church leader in the former Yugoslavia, he was a translator of theological literature, founder and editor of a magazine, and a theological educator. Yet in the portrait my memories had drawn of him, his accomplishments formed only the background. Dominant was his person, not his work. As I was leaving the morgue after having kissed his lifeless body goodbye, I saw more clearly than ever before what an extraordinarily good person he was.

At his memorial service I said, among other things:

My father was one of the best persons I knew. Above all, he was a man of integrity; he practiced what he preached. I can't remember hearing him speak ill of anyone, and he certainly never sang his own praises. He was a humble man who readily admitted his mistakes and asked for forgiveness. I never noticed envy in him nor heard him put down anyone. Although he was a leader, I never saw him manipulate his subordinates. In many ways he was a perfectionist, yet he was thankful for what he had and content with the state he was in.

He was generous; rare was a table prayer in which he did not ask the Lord to give him and his family open hands toward those who suffer want. Finally, there was nothing forced in my father's goodness; he did not try to protect it either by surrounding it with inflexible laws or by pushing others into conformity with himself. Like true holiness, his goodness attracted rather than repelled.

Whenever my father spoke of his father, he always mentioned his extraordinary goodness. My father seems to have inherited that goodness. Born in a shabby little house with a dirt floor in a tiny village called Sirac, he rose to become a prominent church leader, known to many not only in Europe but throughout the world. In his success, however, he never lost the goodness his father had exemplified. My father's greatness lies in that goodness which remained unspoiled by success. Absence of goodness calls into question every success, but nothing, absolutely nothing, calls goodness into question. The greatest compliment one can give to a human being is not that he or she is successful, but that he or she is good. My father deserved that compliment.

When my sabbatical in Germany was over, tombs no longer helped direct the light of the end upon my daily life. But occasionally my disheveled face, after just awakening from a night's rest, would look at me from the mirror and greet: "Remember that you will die!" The next time I hear those words, I'll make them a challenge not so much to what I do, but to who I am. Does doing well not matter then? Yes, it does; but my father's death has reminded me unforgettably that being good matters more. And just as a good tree brings forth good fruit, so being good will take care of doing — or not doing — well.

CHURCH

Not by Sausage Alone

When I was in Croatia this past May I went on a hunt for a sausage. Not just for any kind of sausage, mind you, but for *kulen,* a specialty from a region of Northeast Croatia called Slavonia. If *kulen* could think and feel, it would be insulted by being counted among mere sausages. You can't buy the best ones in any store, of course. To get it you've got to have friends in very high places — in backwater villages of Slavonia where people raise their own pigs and prepare *kulen* according to recipes passed on in families for generations.

A former student of mine has such a friend, and so we got into a car and drove some twenty miles to visit Djeda (or Grandpa) Gjordje, whose *kulen* is supposed to be the best in the region. His was one of those nondescript houses on a nondescript village street with ditches dug along the road as a sewage system. On his house there was no TV antenna, let alone a satellite dish — otherwise ubiquitous in many Croatian towns. As we entered the kitchen, which also functioned as a living room, I saw on the table an open Bible. He was obviously reading it before we came in. As he sat down after welcoming us, he placed his right hand on the table next to the Bible. It was a rough farmer's hand. Just as farm work has left indelible traces on that hand, so that hand has left its mark on the Bible. Its pages, each carefully handled, had obviously been read and reread many times.

After he offered us wine — his product, too! — we started talking. Not about *kulen,* though he knew why we had come, but about Christian life.

"Always choose a more difficult path," Djeda Gjordje offered as a nugget of wisdom at one point in the conversation.

"What do you mean?" responded a neighbor who happened to be there. "If I want to dig a hole in the ground, should I use a dull shovel rather than a sharp one?"

"I didn't mean it that way," said Djeda Gjordje, irritated a bit that his neighbor didn't get what he was after. "It's easier for us to be served than to serve and to take than to give. Serving is the harder path, giving is the harder path. Because we are selfish, the path of love is always more difficult."

I wanted to chime in with reference to Robert Frost and his road "less traveled," but I restrained myself, aware that none of the others would have heard of the poet. And Frost seemed to have been making a different point — one about the possibilities of discovery and the virtues of difference rather than about the nobility of service. So I just listened — and marveled.

I didn't marvel that Djeda Gjordje was wise enough to come up with the idea. That would have been condescending. People aren't any less wise or virtuous because they live in what from a Western standpoint look like primitive surroundings. Rather, I was amazed that we were having that kind of conversation rather than just exchanging a few pleasantries about the weather or sports, or even complaining about corrupt politics and an inefficient economy. But if the Bible is the book you read, your conversations will likely concern the deep questions of life rather than skirt them. Compared with the way most of us spend our evenings in the West, the true marvel was that Djeda Gjordje was the man of one Book. Instead of sinking down in front of a TV or going to the village pub to drink down the hardship and sorrow of his dreary existence with his buddies, evening after evening he read the Bible and meditated on it.

On our way home my driver told me about his American friend's grandfather. After the old man retired at the age of seventy, he spent most of his time glued to the TV watching sports, soap operas, or just channel surfing. The flickering box offered mostly mindless entertainment. It helped him pass time, but it left him empty. There was little to prod him to seek truth, goodness, and beauty. Instead of elevating him, with its glitzy drama that trades on our desire for power, money, sex, and glory, TV pulled him down into the banality of everyday existence.

Rather than feasting on delicious and nutritious specialties like *kulen,* he was feeding on junk food's empty calories.

As I was thinking about Djeda Gjordje and his well-worn Bible, I remembered having heard that in any village in Mauritania, one of the poorest nations in the world, you could find a dozen men able to recite the whole Qur'an by heart. True, unlike most of the Bible, the Qur'an is written in verse, which is easier to remember than prose. But still it takes time to commit such a large book to memory, and to keep it there. On the fringes of what we call civilization, many people take a great deal of time to read texts about great questions of human existence and the challenges of a life worth living.

Over the past decades cultural critics have bemoaned the loss of biblical literacy in the West. Even educated people are unable to understand great classics of Western literature because they are unfamiliar with the Bible, which forms its indispensable background. That's a major cultural loss. But that loss is small compared to the moral, spiritual, and intellectual impoverishment that comes from letting our lives be saturated by the superficial instead of being immersed into the profound.

I went away from Djeda Gjordje's home with two large and superb *kulens* — more than six pounds' worth. His culinary skills were formidable. But as I think of him, I am even more impressed by that open Bible and the conversation it elicited in that remote corner of Croatia.

Way of Life

From this theologian's perspective, the central challenge for pastoral ministry today concerns the most important mark of good ministry: the ability effectively to mediate faith as an integral way of life to persons, communities, and cultures. This has been true throughout history, in every culture and for every community of faith. But in our time maybe more than ever communities of faith seem to be falling short precisely at this point.

If the number of people actively engaged in religious practices were the only relevant indicator, one could think that on the whole communities of faith were as successful today in mediating faith as a way of life as they were decades or even a century ago. And yet the faith that people embrace is, arguably, shaping their lives less and less. Faith seems not so much an integral way of life as an energizing and consoling aura added to the business of a life shaped by factors other than faith.

An indicator of this change is a shift in language to describe religiosity. We have moved away from "faith" to "spirituality." The talk of "faith" rightly emphasizes cognitive and moral content and life in community; the talk of "spirituality," on the other hand, is cognitively and morally vague and emphasizes the empowerment and healing of autonomous individuals.

This increasing difficulty of connecting faith and life stems primarily neither from lack of effort nor from the absence of skills on the part of communities of faith and their leaders. As many sociologists of religion have noted, part of the problem is that in a market society, faith has a difficult time escaping the logic of the marketplace. It is in danger of degenerating into yet another consumer good, to be used when the need for it is felt and placed in storage or discarded when not. The problem is not merely that faith is "bought and sold" as a consumer good (the so-called commodification of religion), but that the smorgasbord culture exerts pressure on people to employ faith to satisfy their discrete and changing wants rather than be the shaper of life as a whole.

The smorgasbord culture is a challenge for communities of faith. But the main problem is that the communities of faith have not found effective ways to offer a compelling vision of an integral way of life that is worth living. Many people are seeking for precisely that, and just because they live in a consumerist culture. They are unsatisfied with a lifestyle shaped only by two watchwords of contemporary culture: "freedom" and "prosperity." This, too, may be signaled by the resurgent interest in spirituality as related to almost every dimension of life — from medicine to business, from arts to politics.

Why do the communities of faith seem ineffective in their central task? The reasons are many, but the difficulty starts with theological education. Like all academic disciplines, theology participates in the movement of subdisciplinary differentiation and increased specialization. This is an indispensable condition of fundamental theological research. In the process, however, the overarching subject of theology and its internal unity seems to get lost. After their first experiences in churches or parachurch organizations, many young pastors are no longer certain that their long years of theological study were useful. The narrowed subjects and highly specialized theological interests of their professors do not sufficiently overlap with the everyday realities of their parishes and parishioners. Three or more years of study have handed them a tool that is sophisticated but of questionable usefulness.

To help themselves out of the predicament, many pastors revert to forms of faith they knew before their theological education began. Some turn to completely uncritical approaches to texts and concepts. These, however, soon prove woefully insufficient for the complexities of life and are intellectually implausible. Others opt for an easy relevance by adopting vague religiosity and interlacing it with various secular languages (for example, of psychology or social critique). These domains of study are valuable in their own right, but in the hands of modern pastors their relation to the language of faith is often tenuous at best. In Michael Welker's apt phrases, the result of these two ways of coping with the difficulty of connecting faith with life is, in the first case, a self-banalization of faith, and in the second, self-secularization. Either of these approaches deprives pastors of the ability to formulate a compelling faith-based vision of life that can shape persons, communities, and cultures.

Pastors can mediate faith as a way of life only if they find it compelling themselves and if their parishioners are moved by it because it makes sense of their lives. For help in defining a compelling faith, ministers have in the past looked to theological institutions of higher learning. It is tragic, however, that even the best of such institutions are producing very little writing about what the Christian faith has to do with the lives of lawyers or artists, manual workers or intellectuals, marketers or politicians, parents or spouses.

One of the most pressing needs of pastoral ministry, therefore, is to develop, sustain, and academically legitimize reflection on Christian faith as a way of life. In the Christian tradition such reflection is not unusual. The most effective and lasting works — of Augustine, Calvin, Luther, Wesley, Kierkegaard, Simone Weil, and others — have been effective and lasting because they offered a vision for a lived faith. Every great theology has been a vision of a way of life. Not surprisingly, the main challenge for pastoral ministry ends up being almost identical to the main challenge for theology and theological education.

Teachers, Crusts, and Toppings

Across the street from Fuller Theological Seminary, where I used to teach, is California Pizza Kitchen. In addition to the traditional cheese and sausage pizzas, it offers such items as Santa Fe Chicken pizza (with tomato salsa and guacamole), Peking Duck pizza (with hoisin sauce), and Tandoori Chicken pizza (with tomato-yogurt curry). The only thing that connects these dishes of Latino, Chinese, and Indian origin with a traditional Italian pizza is the same thing that holds each of them together — a pizza crust.

It occurs to me that the California Pizza Kitchen menu can serve as a good metaphor for contemporary culture: market mechanisms, technology, and communication lines are the crust upon which diverse cultural toppings are placed, side by side and one on top of the other, partly mixed and melted together, partly in discrete chunks, with new combinations replacing the old ones and the old ones reappearing in new forms on popular demand. Student bodies at any theological school could equally well be compared to these pizzas: the common crust of Christian commitments and an institutional framework connects students of radically diverse cultures, denominations, ethnic backgrounds, and convictions.

How do I, a theologian, teach such a student body about Christian tradition and identity? In what sense do I help them develop critical skills? What is the place of the Bible, creeds, and confessions in the teaching setting? With a student body in which Peking Duck and Santa Fe Chicken are offered as pizza dishes on the same menu, there is no single and proper way to approach the task; the task may not even be a single task. Diverse students require diverse approaches. Three examples, typical but not exhaustive, will illustrate.

First, I was lecturing on eschatology. My topic: "The Resurrection of the Body." After I finished, a student from the first row came up to me and confessed: she had never before heard of the resurrection of the body. I was tempted to ask what she was doing in a graduate school class in systematic theology. We are here to grapple with profound issues, I thought, not to learn the theological alphabet. Though I did not ask, she answered: She was a new Christian and this was her very first class in theology. All she brought to seminary besides a good mind and a degree from a prestigious college was a heart warmed by the love of God and a pair of wide-open eyes. She had never read 1 Corinthians 15, never recited the creed. As far as she was concerned, the Bible was unexplored, the Christian tradition *terra incognita*.

Clearly, one of my tasks was and is to teach students to think theologically. Before they can think, however, they must not only know what the tradition says, but also believe that the tradition is worth thinking about. I must therefore draw students — especially those with no Christian socialization — into the world of Christian tradition, teach them the significance of the questions it has sought to answer, and make plausible the answers it has given. They must see the tradition as a viable and attractive way of life before they can start critically reflecting on it; their commitments must be formed and strengthened before a sustained examination of these commitments can make sense. Without a claim of the tradition on them, neither a sympathetic discovery nor a critical rejection will be possible — only inane indifference.

Second, I was lecturing on ecclesiology. My topic: "The Ordination of Women." A student who could not wait until I was finished laying out the biblical and theological bases for why women should be ordained interrupted with a minilecture of his own. It boiled down to the claim that God created Eve in such a way that none of her daughters, under any circumstances, is capable of leading any of Adam's adult sons. This, he assured me, was what the Bible infallibly taught, and this, he added, was what the whole church always and everywhere practiced — until feminism replaced the word of God with the tradition of men.

How does one teach students who are deeply committed to the

Christian way of life, have read a good deal of the Bible and know some of
the tradition, but are locked into misusing the Bible and tradition as
ready-made blueprints for ordering life? If I need to lead the first kind of
students into the tradition, I need to lead this second kind, in a sense, out
of it — that is, out of their own understanding of the tradition and of how
it bears upon life today. Such students need to distance themselves from
the text of the Bible and reflect carefully before they self-righteously exclaim: "It is written." Similarly, I need to teach them to "distance" God
from the text and see both that God is bigger than the text and that the
text, for all its revelatory character, is also a culturally situated message
addressed by one human being to another. Finally, students must learn
to distance both themselves and God from their own subcultures so as to
be able critically to examine those subcultures rather than unsuspect-
ingly read both the Bible and the world through the lenses of those subcultures.

After this exercise in distancing I want the students to return, of
course — to rediscover God in the text, reidentify with the tradition, and
reinsert themselves into their multiple contexts. For without a return,
the distancing remains barren.

Third, a third type of student is increasingly appearing (though very
few students, if any, think of themselves as belonging to this category):
They have sufficient distance from Christian tradition and their particular subculture. They are not dogmatic about their biblical interpretations and do not equate their subculture with the way things ought to be.
To put it sociologically, they are at home in a world of institutionalized
pluralism, variety, contingency, and ambivalence; kaleidoscopic change
is their kind of permanence. For them, the Christian tradition has its
own wisdom, which is sometimes useful and sometimes not, and therefore should sometimes be followed and at other times disregarded.
Whether useful or not, a piece of Christian tradition is but one of many
items in the bustling and ever-changing shopping mall of life.

As a teacher of theology, my task is to take the kaleidoscope apart,
and put inside it a piece so strange that when the students put the kaleidoscope back up to their eye they will exclaim, "Wait a minute, this
shouldn't be here!" I am a guardian of the Christian tradition's alterity, its
otherness. I must teach students not to occlude its opacity, not to distort

87

it by squeezing it into their own cognitive frameworks and by pressing it into their strangely predetermined life of constant change and impermanence of everything. The students must learn not to trivialize the wisdom of the tradition by taking from it only what they happen to need, recycling what they can use in a different form, and disregarding the rest. Critical engagement will be encouraged and angry rejection respected, but domestication will not be tolerated. With alterity lost, teachers and students of theology remain incarcerated within the circle of their own shifting familiarities, incapable of hearing anything but ever-changing echoes of their own voices and the voices of their own culture.

Whatever else an undomesticated Christian tradition may tell us, it is certain to underscore how profoundly different our lives must be from what the image of the shopping malls suggests. Human choices that truly matter are not between chic and tacky but between justice and oppression, not between useful and ornamental but between good and evil, not between expensive and cheap but between life and death, not between voguish and outmoded but between God and idols. Because the Christian tradition teaches about these fundamental choices, it is worth handing it on, worth teaching critical skills to engage it responsibly, worth guarding its alterity, worth doing whatever needs to be done so that the students, whatever mixture of toppings they happen to represent, may learn to discern between enslaving ideologies and the liberating truth of the gospel.

Proclaiming the Lord's Death

H igh view of the ministry of the Word and pronounced free-church sensibilities notwithstanding, I finally caved in. I sought refuge from bad preaching in the celebration of the Eucharist.

My gripe was not with the oratorical skills of preachers in the churches I frequented, though many would have done well to add some rhetorical polish. My problem was not even that sermons were "unbiblical" in the sense that ministers failed to seek inspiration in the scriptures, though some seemed to be commenting on the biblical texts in order to drape their own opinions with the mantle of the prophets' and apostles' authority. More than with rhetoric or the use of the scripture, I was disturbed by the failure of many preachers to make the center of the Christian faith the center of their proclamation. Except in superficial ways, they often kept silent on the topic that should have demanded all their eloquence — Jesus Christ crucified for the ungodly.

Writing to the church in Corinth, the apostle Paul noted that "the message of the cross is foolishness to those who are perishing, but to us who are being saved it is the power of God." Today, however, the message of the cross seems just as foolish to those who should be helping the perishing get saved as it is to the perishing themselves! Many preachers are hesitant to follow the great apostle who decided "to know nothing among" his listeners "except Jesus Christ, and him crucified." Instead, to those who seek wisdom, they offer sapiential musings; to those who demand signs, they give advice on how to transform the world.

Forget about "God's foolishness" which is "wiser than human wisdom," they say implicitly, as they concentrate on, say, putting yesterday's news into perspective or helping people understand this or that psychological hang-up. Forget about "God's weakness" which is "stronger than human strength," they suggest as they zero in on alleviating pressing social needs or curing physical ailments.

My point is not that physical, psychological, and social well-being is unimportant or that the church should remain uninvolved. To the contrary. But if the church's existence were primarily about these issues, a perfectly good argument could be made that on a Sunday morning, instead of going to church, one should get cozy in one's armchair with the *New York Times* in hand and a large mug of cappuccino close by. A morning spent with a good newspaper or book would certainly better prepare one to engage the problems of the world than sitting at the feet of preachers who talk about "wisdom" and "signs."

Fortunately, the choice is not between going to church to hear a sermon or staying at home with a newspaper or book. In church one can also receive the sacrament of the body and blood of Jesus Christ (and pray for a good sermon in addition). Some time ago, Emil Brunner suggested that the sacraments are the best antidote to a minister "who lives by his own wisdom rather than from the scriptures. Even the most audacious minister has not dared to lay hands on the sacraments."

Brunner continues, "One may so interpret the words of scripture that the words speak the opposite of their intent; but the sacraments, thank God, speak a language independent of the language of the Pastor. They are a part of the message of the Church least affected by theological or other tendencies; and that is their special blessing." Brunner may have underestimated the audaciousness of some ministers who feel as entitled to redesign the sacraments as they feel inclined to avoid the cross of Christ. But where the sacraments are left intact, they point straight back to Christ's self-giving on the cross.

Dissatisfied with ministers who live by their own wisdom, I turned to the Eucharist. Its celebration takes participants back to the night on which the Lord of Glory was betrayed and to the day on which his crucified body was suspended between the heavens and the earth. Its "special blessing" lies in not letting us forget that Christians' lives rest on Christ's body given and his blood spilled and that their calling is to "live in love, as Christ loved us and gave himself up for us, a fragrant offering and sacrifice to God." In the celebration of the Eucharist the church receives itself anew by the power of the Holy Spirit as that which it is and ought to be — the body of Christ given for the salvation of the world. Augustine put it beautifully to his congregation: "So if it's you that are the body of Christ and its members, it's the mystery meaning you that has been placed on the Lord's table; what you receive is the mystery that means you. It is to what you are that you reply Amen, and by so replying you express your assent."

The gathering of believers is the place where by the power of the Spirit and through the celebration of the Eucharist we are made into the body of Christ — for our own salvation and for the salvation of the world. And so on any Sunday morning I happily leave my newspaper at home and head for a church whose primary purpose is neither to enlighten nor empower me, but "to proclaim the Lord's death until he comes."

Will the stress on the Eucharist produce a church withdrawn from public engagement? It could. But it need not. Indeed, as William T. Cavanaugh argues in his fascinating book *Torture and Eucharist* (1998), a proper celebration of the Eucharist is a liturgically enacted counter-politics to the politics of this world. By drawing the church back to the cross of Christ, the Eucharist furnishes the church with resources to resist the injustice, deceitfulness, and violence that mark the world for which Christ died.

Is It God's Business?

A Presbyterian minister told me a story about his first year at a certain congregation. His predecessor had abolished the general confession of sins from the Sunday liturgy, and one of the first things this new pastor did was try to reinstate it. But resistance to the proposed change was fierce. Some members thought that confession of sins was too morbid a thing to do in church, where one's spirits were supposed to be lifted up.

During the heat of the debate one woman — an elder — exclaimed, "But I don't have to apologize to God for anything!" The pastor was dumbfounded. "My seminary training hadn't prepared me for this," he told me. Whether we are pastors or teachers of future pastors, we usually find the need for confession so obvious that we don't even bother to inquire as to why we might have to "apologize to God."

I can only guess what that elder meant by her startling denial. She might have meant that God should be bothered only with grave sins such as murder or adultery. Since she had not committed any of these, she did not need to apologize to God. Smaller sins are like traffic violations: one pays for them where payment is due, and that's the end of it.

The response to such a line of thinking would be simple: Anger is God's concern as much as murder, lust as much as adultery. Though it may be helpful to differentiate between big and small sins in relation to their impact upon the sinner herself and her neighbors, all sins, no matter how small, are God's concern.

Or she might have meant that her initial faith and baptism had granted her absolution for all the sins she had ever committed and could ever possibly commit. As far as God is concerned, she might have been thinking, everything has already been taken care of. In this case the response would be a bit more complicated: our sins cannot be fully "taken care" of in advance, for the simple reason that forgiveness needs to be received and not just given, that it requires our self-awareness as those who have sinned, and self-awareness in turn requires the naming of acts that we have committed as sins.

There is yet another way we might interpret the elder's comment. "An apology is due to a person against whom one has transgressed," she might have been thinking. "When I transgress against my neighbor, I go to her, apologize, and make the necessary amends. And since for the most part I never really encounter God, let alone transgress against God, why would I need to apologize to God? God is in heaven and I am on earth. Whoever storms heaven to injure God's divine highness, let him apologize. My sins are of a more modest kind, all directed against creatures here below, and all to be ironed out between ourselves."

A theologian could jump in: "But you don't seem to understand what sin means. Sin is fundamentally a *theological* category; by definition, every sin is a sin against God, no matter who else is involved. Take God out of it, and our small and large deceptions and injustices are just that: deceptions, injustices, and violences; but they are not sins."

"That's just what I would expect a theologian to say," she might counter. "Let's not quibble about definitions; let's look at the matter itself. Surely the question is not how one defines sin, but why acts which have nothing to do with God should be deemed sins. If I cheat on my husband, I've cheated on my husband; I haven't done God any wrong. Why should I apologize to God for what I have done to my husband?" And to prevent the theologian from making a quick rejoinder, she could add, "Don't tell me that I should not cheat because God commands me not to do so. For then God would be like a parent whose pride gets the better of her. She demands obedience to her commands just because they are her commands."

This is where things get complicated — and interesting. "At one level," the theologian might respond, "sin is a transgression against God's command. But a transgression against God's command is not just a sin because it is an act of disobedience. The trouble has started already when one thinks of God as being 'out there' and of us as being 'down here.' God is not just 'in heaven'; God is also 'on earth.' The earth and all that is in it are God's, in a way a teddy bear is a child's. Their well-being is God's joy; their pain is God's suffering. When you transgress against your neighbor, it involves God, because you are transgressing against one of God's creatures and therefore against God. In relation to our transgressions, God is not simply a just and all-knowing referee who remains outside these purely human disputes. God is always also an injured party. For every transgression against the neighbor, apology is owed both to the neighbor and to God.

"Which is why" — and here our imaginary dialogue returns to the original issue — "the confession of sins is appropriately included in services of Christian worship. It is in worship that together we meet the God who is not simply enthroned in heaven 'out there' untouched by anything we do, but also 'down here,' a lover of creation, concerned with the sufferings of creation. And in worship we meet God who 'dwells with us,' supremely in the person of Jesus Christ, and who thereby receives our acknowledgment of wrongdoing and pronounces us forgiven; and it is in this community that we can learn the hard work of reconciliation and renewal in the power of God's Spirit given to us."

Not, perhaps, very different from what one would expect a theologian to say. But then occasionally a theologian may be right even when he says what we expect him to say.

Reflected Light

This past summer, at our family home in Croatia, I was immersed in George Weigel's long biography of the late John Paul II, *Witness to Hope*. As the intense focus of world attention on his funeral made plain, he was one of very few contemporary world leaders in the true sense of that word. In many regards he was a global moral conscience. That was plain for all to see during his life and even more clearly after he died. But what I had not realized until reading the book was that he considered holiness to be the prime qualification of a priest. By being "holy" he did not mean standing aloof from others, nose in the air, and urging them to shape up by pointing to one's own alleged superior qualities. Holy people are those who are transparent before the loving God and who give themselves in love to their neighbors. All his limitations notwithstanding, if we are to believe his closest friends, he lived what he preached more consistently than most of us.

As I was reading about the saintly John Paul II, a friend gave me a book by a first-time Croatian author eager to "see what I thought about it." The book's genre is that of a novel, and the novel is a love story. But it is written in the first person singular and is in fact a true confession. After a divorce, a young successful atheist lawyer is left with a small son and a search for meaning — with the desire to "touch that ground out of which everything grows." She enters a church about which she doesn't know very much, thinking that a priest may be able to help her. She finds a dynamic, progressive priest, falls in love, and for more than a decade lives as his secret lover. She is pulled into his world while continuing with her own career, studies theology for a year, and eventually starts writing sermons for him.

Gradually she comes to realize that something is profoundly wrong with the priest and her relationship to him. For he is not just a celibate priest who has, in a moment of weakness, slipped up on the chastity part of his priestly vows. A minister of God, he is interested only in worldly power and wealth and in women and wine. A servant of people, he despises them as rabble that ought to be exploited rather than helped. The woman participates in all this because she loves the man. Yet the more she reads the Bible the more uncomfortable she becomes. Living in the midst of hypocrisy, she is attracted to truth; living with a religious manipulator, she longs for the God of grace. In what must be one of the strangest conversions ever to happen, she encounters the living God by writing sermons for her hypocritical lover.

I was glued to the book, which is written under the pseudonym Eta Lodi to preserve the privacy of the people involved (including the author, who is a prominent judge in Croatia). At one level, the book is a love story in which a narrative of forbidden love with a failed "man of God" culminates in the discovery of the true Lover. As I was reading it, I was pulled by the unpredictable journey of the author's desire — desire for love, for meaning, and ultimately for God. At this level, the author itself is the main character of her story.

At another level, the book is a critique of false religiosity. The priest in question is not simply an individual person; he stands for the whole system of institutionalized religiosity, a system drained of authentic Christian faith, in which custom and ritual serve as a cover for religious nakedness and as justification for exploiting simple folk. The book is also a critique of obligatory celibacy for priests. It exposes from within a subterranean world of people who take on holy orders but are unable to fulfill their own commitments and, unless they are willing to give up on their vocation, are forced to live double lives to their own and their flock's detriment. At this second level, the author is less of a lover than a prophet and the corrupt priest is the main character.

I read the story primarily at yet another level — with God as the main character. It is a story of the power of the Gospel in the midst of corrupt people and religious institutions. As I read the book, I thought of a line in one of Job's speeches. Addressing God, he asks rhetorically, "Who can bring what is pure from the impure?" (14:4). The response is, obviously: "No one but God." Impure was the well to which Eta Lodi, thirsty for God, came to drink. And yet notwithstanding the mud of a corrupt priestly life and the strange concoctions of his sub-Christian teaching, she still found through him the spring of pure and living water! Which brings us back to John Paul II and his call for priestly holiness.

Is priestly holiness superfluous when God can work through unholy men and women (and sometimes does *not* seem to work through *holy* men and women!)? Obviously, it is not. A life of genuine holiness is what God desires to create in individuals and churches, because that life is a reflection of God's own life in humanity. But Eta Lodi's story reminds us that the passing on of Christian faith is not primarily a matter of anything human beings do, not even primarily a matter of any holiness that we exhibit (or, as we like to say now, of our excellent practices). Instead, Christian faith is always a gift of God's life-changing presence.

"The Light shines in the darkness," writes John the Evangelist. Whether it is the light that comes to us through God's holy people or the light that shines more directly into our hearts, it is always God's light and not human light. Indeed, any true light that we humans might have at all will always be, like the moon's, a reflected light.

Changing and Changeless

The theology of Cardinal Joseph Ratzinger, now Pope Benedict XVI, played a major part in my book *After Our Likeness* (1998), which sought to develop a Trinitarian, nonhierarchical understanding of the church. He thanked me politely for the copy I sent him and added, "You don't expect me, of course, to have changed my mind after reading it."

I had no such expectation. I am a Protestant in the bewildering world of restless spiritual energy splashing from below, in the world of multiplying churches, small and large, traditional and contemporary. He was then the guardian of orthodoxy and the second-ranking person in the Catholic Church, the body whose distinctive mark is visible social unity. I was advocating for new and emerging churches, while he was trying to keep them from making inroads among his flock.

In the debates that raged about the fate of the Second Vatican Council, Ratzinger parted ways with his erstwhile friends, such as the progressive theologian Hans Küng. They insisted that he was busy closing the windows of the church which Vatican II had opened. He snapped back that he had not changed; instead, they had changed by swallowing modernity hook, line, and sinker, abandoning the substance of the faith in the process.

From 1954, when he published his first book, until the present day, the new pope's theology has remained amazingly consistent. At its heart is the idea of "communion" — the communion of God with humans and of humans with one another, in the one body of the church. What makes communion possible? The utter transparency of each person to God, as exemplified by Christ, and self-giving love for one's neighbor. This, roughly, is the new pope's spirituality.

Now, apply this spirituality to the papacy. Though he is the Supreme Pontiff, according to Ratzinger the pope is nothing as an individual. His presence doesn't matter; God's presence does. His personal beliefs don't matter; the one faith of the church does. Like Jesus, the pope should say, "My teaching is not my own, but of the One who sent me." And that commitment to something that is neither one's own nor at one's disposal brings us back to the question of change.

Semper idem — always the same — is what the Catholic Church has traditionally said of itself. The world today is awhirl with change, however. One gadget is pushing the other to the garbage heap; one fad is replacing another at breathless speed; knowledge is accumulating exponentially; old political structures are breaking down and fresh ones are being erected. As new things give way to the *new* new things, can the Catholic Church afford to remain changeless? If it does not change, could it be abandoned like a car from three decades ago or driven only on a rare Sunday morning as a well-preserved antique? On the other hand, with the obsolescence rate so high, can the church afford to keep changing? If today it marries the spirit of a breathless age, will it not become a widow tomorrow? The church must do both: hold onto the substance of the faith while finding ever new ways to express it.

Semper idem is what we should expect Joseph Ratzinger to say at the end of his pontificate as Benedict XVI. As a pope, will he be wise enough to differentiate rightly between the self-same substance of faith and its many and changing expressions? That is the crucial question of this papacy.

In the 1990s, when I was involved in a dialogue with the Pontifical Council for Promoting Christian Unity, a German Vatican insider friend and I were musing about the possibility of a German pope, with a side glance toward Cardinal Ratzinger. "A German wouldn't make a good pope," he said. "Why not?" I asked. "We Germans are too rigid," he replied. "We take ourselves and our jobs too seriously, and the church is a very diverse and living body."

Can Benedict XVI prove my friend wrong? Can a stern watchdog morph into an embracing shepherd? These questions are, however, not just for a new pope to answer. They concern every Christian. Can we, whether pastors, lay people, or theologians, live authentically a changeless Gospel in ever-changing cultures?

Ecumenical Quandary

Recently Yale Divinity School organized a conference to mark a major ecumenical event of the 1990s (some would even argue the major ecumenical event of the last century). It was the signing of the *Joint Declaration on the Doctrine of Justification* by the Lutheran World Federation and the Roman Catholic Church. The declaration affirms "a consensus on basic truths on the doctrine of justification" and claims "that the remaining differences in its explication are no longer the occasion for doctrinal condemnations." With the signing, an important bridge has been built across a rift that divided Western Christendom for almost five hundred years.

As I was preparing for the conference, I was reminded of the raging debates in Germany about the text of the declaration. After the final draft was sent to the churches for consideration, some one hundred forty Protestant theology professors publicly opposed it. Since the Vatican's Congregation for the Doctrine of the Faith was also displeased, an Annex was prepared. Although Rome and some prominent Protestant theologians considered the Annex a marked improvement over the main text, an even greater number of theologians rose up against it. At the bottom of an appeal urging the Lutheran World Federation not to sign the declaration with the Annex, one could read the names of more than two hundred thirty German theologians who belong to groups that otherwise have almost nothing in common. Moreover, the debates about the issue were not limited to theological faculties and churches. Some of the most prominent newspapers in the German-speaking world participated vigorously.

No such uproar over the declaration took place in the United States. For all I can tell, discussions among theologians were limited to a relatively narrow circle of ecumenical activists who thought the declaration a great success. But the wider public hardly registered the event. In general, there was neither criticism nor celebration of the declaration. Its advent was greeted with the silence of indifference.

The vehemence of the debates in Germany can partly be explained by the fact that Germany is the land of the Reformation. But why a yawn of indifference elsewhere? I want to suggest two reasons, one that concerns general culture in late capitalist societies and the other that concerns developments in Protestant Christianity.

First, wide segments of the population in Western cultures increasingly deem debates about religious doctrines to be insignificant. The problem is not primarily that life has run ahead of a particular set of beliefs, so that they no longer seem relevant. Rather, doctrines as such have lost importance. Flexible "options" and shifting "feelings" about things are increasingly replacing strong convictions with a claim to truth. People today tend to think that only bigots argue about the truth of their religious beliefs.

Second, for some years now established Protestant denominations have been declining numerically, losing social influence, and undergoing an identity crisis. Within Protestantism, numerical growth and spiritual dynamism seem to have migrated to evangelicals, Pentecostals, and charismatics, especially in non-Western countries. Pentecostals and charismatics have a larger membership than all the Protestant denominations combined: they represent the second largest body in Christendom. And there are no signs that their growth is slowing down. Hundreds of new churches are being born daily.

The significance of these two trends for the future of ecumenism becomes obvious as soon as one remembers the character of ecumenical work as practiced over the past fifty years. The way the declaration about justification was forged is a good example. It took thirty years of painstaking work in numerous national and international settings. And the work is by no means done. Once the document is finished, the process of its ecclesial reception begins — with uncertain results, as the "rebellion" of German theologians shows. Add to this that the document addresses only one issue that divides Catholic and Lutheran churches, even if the issue is the most important one. After a staggering magnitude of work, ecumenical progress has come at a snail's pace.

The most significant challenge for ecumenical efforts stems from the clash between the nature of ecumenical processes and powerful cultural and ecclesial developments. Just think: In the time it takes for ecumenical agreement to be reached on just one doctrine, dozens of new denominations and thousands of loosely associated congregations will emerge worldwide with a multimillion membership! All the ecumenical running notwithstanding, we will continue to fall behind.

One way to address the problem would be to replace an ecumenism of theological dialogues with an ecumenism of practical cooperation. But this will not do. On critical issues, churches find it as difficult to work together as they have to believe together. After all, as the difficulties in forging common action-statements in relation to the global economic system or the issues of sexuality show, in the absence of shared *beliefs* it is not easy to agree on what is to be *done*. Doctrines matter, and one major theological task is to help churches understand why.

We can neither abandon an ecumenism of dialogues nor rest satisfied with it. How to get past this quandary is the most important problem facing the ecumenical movement today. The crisis of ecumenical institutions is real (as debates about the survival and shape of the National Council of Churches in the U.S.A. or the World Council of Churches globally attest), and it demands our attention. But we will hardly be able to create healthy institutions if we are unclear about the very nature of the ecumenical work that will be required in the future.

Mission and Other Faiths

Urban Mission

When I visited a Baltimore neighborhood called Sandtown in 1997, my most vivid impression was that of disturbing, jarring contrast. I remember a whole neighborhood of abandoned houses — each one an oversized skull, with empty darkness peering out of its broken doors and windows and mocking the life that had abandoned it. In the midst of these ruins, however, there was a street teeming with life. Houses had been repaired and painted with bright colors, neighbors were chatting, children were playing in the street. It was as though in this one place a resurrection of sorts had clothed the dry bones of urban death with the pulsating flesh of life. At the heart of this improbable transformation was a small company of Christians. They call themselves the New Song Community.

To Live in Peace (2002) tells the story of this community and offers a theological rationale for its mission in the inner city. Author Mark Gornik, responding to a call from God, was among the first to relocate to Sandtown. The book gives eloquent testimony to lives modeled on Christ's self-giving love and inspired by the Spirit of life — lives that here transform hopeless urban landscapes into sites of God's peace.

To read this book properly, jump straight to Chapter 5, "Singing a New Song." This, the story of Sandtown's gradual "resurrection," is the book's heart. Without it, the important theological and sociological reflections that precede and follow cannot be properly understood. Inspired by John Perkins's pioneering work in community development (his famous "three Rs": relocation, reconciliation, redistribution), Gornik and Allan Tibbles moved into the neighborhood armed with no "plans or programs," but only the conviction that "the church is God's reconciled community pursuing justice at the point of greatest suffering in the world."

They started by hanging around in the community until, in a testimony "to Sandtown's capacity for grace," they were welcomed. From then on, as Gornik puts it, everything was not so much an effort of the few who relocated to Sandtown, but of the many who didn't abandon it "during hard times." First came a community church, then homes affordable for everyone, then drastic improvement of the local educational system and health care. Finally an effective employment strategy was put into place. Achievements are easy to enumerate, but every successful step required a miracle of courage and persistence.

I went away from the book moved and challenged in many ways. First is a *personal* challenge. Gornik and Tibbles chose not to pursue the comforts of ministry in middle-class environments. Instead, they relocated to a place of desolation and hopelessness. For Tibbles this was a special challenge: he is a quadriplegic, married, and a father of two girls. What struck me was not just a robust sainthood of the two men, but how lightly they were wearing it, without effort or self-importance.

Second is an *ecclesial* challenge. Notwithstanding the rhetoric of service to the world, churches often succumb to the temptation to live primarily for themselves — to increase their numbers, improve their programs, add new buildings. For the New Song Community, being the church means being for others, with others, especially the neediest. "The ministries of justice and reconciliation are not additions that flow out of the church," but are "constitutive of ecclesial life in union with Christ."

The third challenge concerns the *character of service.* All too often we help the needy in a way that humiliates them. Even talk about "empowerment" leaves a bitter taste of condescension. *To Live in Peace* is suffused with deep respect for the dignity of the needy. They are not the "others" for whom something must be done, even less the ignorant who must be taught or the unruly who must be disciplined. They are the family members who have fallen on hard times and must be encouraged and helped.

Fourth, the challenge of *connecting faith with life.* Gornik argues repeatedly against approaching the problem of the inner cities with ready blueprints either derived from faith or informed by secular reasoning (although in the book he does a great deal of theological and sociological heavy-lifting). Instead, he suggests a twofold strategy: (1) keep focused on the vision toward which the community needs to move (the *shalom* of God's new creation) and on the path on which it needs to walk (Christ's self-giving love), and (2) concentrate "upon faithfully doing thousands of little things right over a period of many years."

Finally, the book is a challenge to how we think about faith-based initiatives. Gornik knows that the church has significant and unique resources for addressing the needs of inner cities; his whole book is an explication of these resources. Yet he cautions that the current emphasis on faith-based initiatives overly personalizes poverty and social change and disregards both "the needs for infrastructure and capital" and the structural dimension of poverty. Gornik refuses to be caught in false alternatives — either attention to persons or to structures. Both need to be addressed if communities are to live in peace, and therefore both the church and the government have a role to play.

The Christian wisdom, commitment, and courage inscribed in Gornik's book and incarnate in the New Song Community are extraordinary. I hope we all will catch something of Gornik's vision: "Guided by the conviction that Christ crucified creates room for the embrace of others and that the Spirit of the resurrected Christ brings new life," the churches can and must serve "to advance the *shalom* of American inner cities."

Sharing Wisdom

We live in an age of petty hopes and persistent conflicts.

Take first our hopes. In the book *The Real American Dream*, Andrew Delbanco traced the history of the scope of American dreams — from the "holy God" of the Puritan founders, to the "great nation" of the nineteenth-century patriots, to the "satisfied self" of many today. With some modifications, America may be in this regard indicative of trends in most societies that are highly integrated into the global market system. The idea of flourishing as a human being has shriveled to meaning no more than leading an experientially satisfying life. The sources of satisfaction may vary: power, possessions, love, religion, sex, food, drugs — whatever. What matters the most is not the *source* of satisfaction but the *experience* of it — *my* satisfaction. Our satisfied self is our best hope. This is not just petty; a dark shadow of disappointment stubbornly follows this obsession with personal satisfaction as well. We are meant to live for something larger than our own satisfied selves. Petty hopes generate self-subverting, melancholy experiences.

Second, our world is caught in great conflicts (as well as in many small, even petty ones). Mostly these conflicts are fought along religious lines. Christians and Muslims are clashing; so are Muslims and Jews, Hindus and Christians, Buddhists and Muslims, and so on. Though for the most part religions per se are not the causes of these conflicts, often religions legitimize and fuel them by enveloping mundane causes — mostly our petty hopes — with an aura of the sacred.

Most religions see as one of their main goals the opening up of self-absorbed individuals to connect them with a broader community and, indeed, with the source and goal of all reality. The Christian faith certainly does. Similarly, most religions claim to contain important, even indispensable resources for fostering a culture of peace. But these two functions of religions are often at odds with one another. When religions connect people with the divine, bring people together, and offer them a hope larger than mere self-fulfillment, communities with differing religious beliefs sometimes clash. When religions try to avoid legitimizing and fueling clashes between people, they often retreat into some private sphere and at times even reinforce people's self-absorption.

Here is a central challenge for all religions in a pluralistic world: Help people grow out of their petty hopes so as to live meaningful lives, and help them resolve their many small and large conflicts and live in communion with others, and do both at the same time. That's where the importance of learning to share religious wisdom well comes in. If we as religious people fail to share wisdom well, we will fail both our many contemporaries who strive to live satisfied lives yet remain deeply dissatisfied, and we will fail those who draw on their religious traditions to give meaning to their lives yet remain mired in intractable and often deadly conflicts.

But how do we share religious wisdom well? Each religious tradition will have to give its own answer to this question, as well as seek to learn from others in the process of answering it. Here are some elements of the art of sharing religious wisdom as they appear from a Christian perspective. They assume that for Christians true wisdom is inseparable from Jesus Christ and that in a fundamental sense it is identical with him.

As Christians, how should we share religious wisdom so as not to deepen conflicts between people? We need to resist the temptation to "help" wisdom gain a footing in people's lives by manipulating or forcing others to embrace wisdom. Similarly, we need to resist the lure of pridefully perceiving ourselves as only givers of wisdom, rather than always also its receivers — and receivers from both expected and unexpected sources. If we give in to these tendencies, we will add to religious conflicts rather than preparing the soil in which religious faith can help resolve them. From a Christian perspective, all our efforts at sharing wisdom should focus on allowing wisdom to shape our own lives and show itself in all its attractiveness, reasonableness, and usefulness. We need to trust that it will make itself embraceable by others if it is going to be embraced at all. In that way, as sharers of wisdom we honor both the power of wisdom and the integrity of its potential recipients.

How should we share wisdom so as not to feed petty hopes but instead help persons connect meaningfully with communities — small and large — and with God as the source and goal of the universe? We need to resist the temptation to "package" religious wisdom in attractive and digestible "nuggets" that a person can take up and insert into some doomed project of striving to live a merely experientially satisfying life. If we don't resist that temptation, we will make wisdom into a servant of folly. From a Christian perspective, sharing religious wisdom makes sense only if that wisdom is allowed to counter the multiple manifestations of human self-absorption and to connect human beings with what ultimately matters — God, whom we should love with all our being, and neighbors, whom we should love as ourselves.

Sikh Wisdom

O ne of the most recognizable pieces of religious architecture in the world is the Golden Temple in Amritsar, India, the most significant place of worship of the Sikhs. The upper part of this ornate rectangular marble structure is covered in gold. I saw the gleaming temple early in the morning, before sunrise, when it was bathed in soft artificial light. It stood immovable as a huge gilded rock, its reflected image dancing gently on the surface of the surrounding pool.

I was in Amritsar as a Christian consultant for a meeting of the Elijah Board of World Religious Leaders, organized by my friend Rabbi Alon Goshen-Gottstein. I had written a position paper to serve as a basis for discussions that would include the Dalai Lama and the chief rabbi of Haifa. Six writers of position papers representing different world religions had discussed their drafts with one another and with a larger interfaith group of scholars. It was a fascinating exercise. As I was writing, I was aided by wisdom from other faith traditions. What I presented as genuinely my own was in part received from others.

I grew up solidly Protestant in an overwhelmingly Catholic and Orthodox environment controlled by aggressively secular communists. Unlike the communists, those in our Protestant tribe nurtured a sense of the holy. But we differed from the Catholics and the Orthodox in that for us holiness was not to be located in time and space. The eternal and omnipresent God was holy; people could be holy if they made themselves available for God; times and places were not holy. We did not follow a liturgical calendar closely, and we met for worship in remodeled rooms of an ordinary house on an ordinary street. As a child of a pastor, I lived in that house; the neighbor kids and I played soccer in its yard and marbles on the patch of dirt in front of it. As examples of sacred architecture, the places where I experienced God — in restless rebellion and not just in sweet surrender — were the polar opposites of the Golden Temple.

At the temple I walked barefoot and with covered head around the holy pool in which people took ritual baths. I observed the people quietly streaming to the temple and walking by the place where *Sri Guru Granth Sahib Ji* is kept, the holy book which ultimately makes the place holy. But I didn't feel spiritually pulled in. I was a sympathetic observer, learning, questioning, puzzling over things, appreciating. I remained an outsider, not a participant.

Yet I took with me something unforgettable, a nugget of enacted religious wisdom that I cherish more than I would a piece of that temple's gold.

The next day, as I walked one more time within the temple complex, I wanted to buy a souvenir for my two boys. Then it dawned on me: I hadn't seen a vendor or a shop anywhere on the temple premises. "Thousands of religious tourists mill around here every day," I thought. "There *must* be a place to buy souvenirs!" But there wasn't.

You had to leave the temple complex and step onto the profane ground of surrounding streets to satisfy your tourist appetite. There peddlers were as busy as anywhere else in the world, and I found what I was looking for — a small kirpan, a ritual sword that all baptized Sikh wear. But not on the holy site — there the only commercial transaction that took place was the purchase of a "ticket" to walk across the bridge to the temple in the middle of the lake. The ticket was a bowl of porridge, the size of which depended on how much you paid. You could eat some of it, but you were expected to put at least a portion of it into large bowls. When the bowls were filled, they were carried off to feed the poor.

The contrast between the Golden Temple and other religious sites I've seen could not be greater. Everywhere else, greedy people — often religious leaders with business managers — were trying to cash in on the devotion of visitors. Here that devotion was channeled into feeding the hungry. I was reminded of the story of Jesus' cleansing of the temple, recorded in all four Gospels. "And he entered the temple and began to drive out those who were selling and those who were buying in the temple. . . .

'Is it not written,' he said, '"My house shall be called a house of prayer for all the nations"? But you have made it a den of robbers.'" The Gospels consistently tie Jesus' death to the cleansing of the temple. Mark's account continues, "And when the chief priests and the scribes heard it, they kept looking for a way to kill him."

I came away from the Golden Temple with a nugget of wisdom — houses of worship should not be sites of commercial activity, but places of gift giving to the needy, just as faith itself is not to be bought and sold but freely given. That Sikh wisdom turned out to be buried treasure of my own faith.

Unaggressive Evangelism

In a lecture I once gave at a small Midwestern college, my topic, broadly put, was encounter with "the other." In a discussion afterwards, a student suggested that engaging in evangelism and seeking to convert another person to the Christian faith is a form of violence, a form of harmful disrespect for the other. Although this opinion is prevalent in certain academic and religious circles, I had not expected it to have traveled so far, culturally speaking. After all, the college where I was speaking was a flagship institution of a denomination known for its evangelistic and missionary efforts.

Undisputedly, some forms of evangelism *are* violent. This holds true for conversions extracted at the point of the sword, a method that brought large parts of Europe into the fold of the church. Less violent but still clearly objectionable are all manipulative methods practiced by overzealous evangelists, be they those who come knocking at our doors or some of those whose faces we see on TV screens. The relevant question is not whether evangelism can be violent; it has been and sometimes is still violent. The question is rather whether evangelism is *inherently* violent.

I posed this last question to a good friend who has engaged in cross-cultural evangelism for years as he works among the so-called "unreached peoples." "What do you think of this objection to your work?" I teased him. "Can you sleep peacefully at night after perpetrating so much violence?" Three things in his response seem particularly significant.

"First," he said, "it all depends how one understands evangelism. I never saw myself endeavoring to convert anyone. God converts. I witness. The main task as a witness is to help people acquire an accurate understanding of the Christian faith. If they reject it, they should not be rejecting its caricatures; if they embrace it, they should know what they are embracing."

"Do you mean that it is wrong to try to persuade people that they ought to embrace the Christian faith? Or do you think it is wrong to somehow seek to make them, in your case, follow Christ?" I asked.

"The latter. If you don't manipulate, persuasion is legitimate, but not effective. I found it best simply to keep removing obstacles and let God nudge people to embark upon the Christian journey. If they understand what the Christian faith is about and still want to reject it, that's their perfect right."

The second point my friend made underscored that seeking to persuade as well as to inform someone of the truth of your religious beliefs, though possibly ineffective, is not inherently violent. "I was more often the evangelized than the evangelizer. The people with whom I lived were very religious. They sought to convince me to follow their religious path. But I did not feel at all violated by their efforts."

"That's interesting," I responded. "Let me venture a guess. For them and for you, religions are not just a matter of different lifestyles, something vaguely analogous to a preference for one ethnic dish over another. Rather, religions make truth claims about what constitutes the good life. So if a Muslim is trying to persuade you to embrace Islam, he is not so much meddling in your private affairs as honoring you as a person to whom truth matters. If he had no desire for you to become a Muslim, you could rightly protest that he was either indifferent to your well-being or to his own faith."

"Yes, although one may still, for other reasons, prefer not to seek to persuade the other of the truth of Islam or Christianity, but simply to offer accurate information. And when it comes to offering such information," my friend said, "there is a third point to make. That's the question of rights. Every person has the right to accurate information about another religion. A person may not claim that right because she doesn't care, but if she does, she has the right to be informed. The only adequate way to inform her about religious beliefs and practices is through representatives of that other religion."

"You mean this as a positive right, like the right to work for the un-employed, the right to social help for the poor?"

"Yes. The U.N. Declaration on Human Rights mentions negative rights, which secure a sphere of freedom, as well as positive rights, which secure essential goods."

"I might easily agree with you that there are such things as positive rights," I responded. "I am just not sure that accurate information about other religions is such a right."

We went on to debate the distinction between negative and positive rights, the role of the state in each case, and how such rights apply to information about religions. The upshot was that we disagreed. I would grant only that those who are interested in another religion have the right to seek that information and that those who want to provide it have the right to give it. He, on the other hand, insisted on the recipients' positive right to have such information made available to them.

But whether one agrees with my friend's stronger or my weaker application of human rights to the issue, the consequences for the student's question are significant. Those providing information about another religious path and persuading seekers of its truth are not violent — provided they agree that actually changing people's allegiances is God's task and not theirs. It is those who want to hinder people from offering and accessing adequate information about other religious paths and questioning the truth of those paths who are violent.

116

Sheep, Wolves, and Doves

"More Christians have been martyred in the 20th century than in the previous centuries combined." As I read this astounding sentence in an e-mail communication about the International Day of Prayer for Persecuted Christians (November 16), my mind went back to an event a few months earlier. I was participating in a talk show on National Public Radio about religious freedom and persecution. The other participants were a Jewish rabbi and a Muslim medical doctor. Congress had just published its report on the issue, and its focus was on Christians. We were asked this question: Should the United States government impose economic and political sanctions on governments that egregiously violate the basic religious rights of Christians?

Early on in the show I had made it clear that I was in favor of focusing on Christians today only if we commit ourselves to focus on other religious groups tomorrow. The persecution of Christians is no greater a crime than the persecution of Jews or Muslims; given our historical legacy, Christians may in fact be well advised to be more outraged at the persecution of adherents of other religions than of their own. I also worried out loud about whether the concern for persecuted Christians will only confirm to some segments of the wider culture that, now that communism is dead, Islam is the new global villain. Will the focus on the evil other out there draw attention away from the evil self right here?

But what about sanctions? I was for them, I said — to the slight surprise of my interlocutors. "But sanctions do not work!" "Well, I've seen them work," I responded, "and even when they don't work, they send an important moral signal." The host dissented and suggested that political wisdom may call us to be more circumspect and patient with some governments — China, for example. "Yeah, right," I snapped back, coating a flash of indignation with irony. "We should be gentle with tyrants with bloody hands." Was I right?

As it happened, the message about the International Day of Prayer for Persecuted Christians came on a morning I was preparing to lecture on martyrdom. On my desk was Erik Peterson's essay on the topic "The Witness to the Truth." In the first paragraph he reminds his readers that the altars of many European churches were built on the bones of the martyrs. "The church is built on the foundation of martyrs," he explains.

The apostles are more important than martyrs, he concedes, but the apostles themselves were called to martyrdom. The account of the call and the sending of the Twelve in the Gospel of Matthew is unambiguous: "See, I am sending you out like sheep into the midst of wolves; so be wise as serpents and innocent as doves."

Peterson's quote prompted me to read the whole text of Matthew 10. No, it does not say the disciples will occasionally fall into the midst of the wolves; it says they are *sent* there. No, it does not say their suffering is a rare anomaly; it is the *rule*. The pattern of suffering was established before they came along. They were called to suffering because they were called to follow the one who suffered. "Whoever does not take up the cross and follow me is not worthy of me."

And then to top it all, the text elevates the suffering of the teacher and the follower to a principle: "Those who find their life will lose it, and those who lose their life for my sake will find it." For the disciples just like for Jesus, there is no uncontested space, no exit from the struggle, and therefore no way to avoid suffering. This is partly why Martin Luther insisted that suffering is in fact a *mark* of the true church, not just an occasional and unfortunate occurrence in its life.

Even more disturbing than the inescapability of suffering is the demand placed on the persecuted. "So be innocent as doves." Yes, I have omitted the injunction to be wise as serpents. Rare is a human sheep living among human wolves who does not quickly learn serpentine ways. Most of us tend to be less fascinated by doves than by serpents. Innocence does not attract us, and when it does, it is difficult to achieve — especially when one's life is at stake.

Even during a friendly exchange with my radio host in the safety of a recording studio, there was an edge to my tone as I spoke of fighting the tyrants. It was not what I said that bothered me; it was how I said it. Vengefulness and even hatred had sneaked up and invaded my indignation. Petty scruples on my part? Maybe. But I was disturbed at sensing a kind of noninnocence surfacing that, in a different setting, could maybe transform me, a presumed sheep, into a rapacious wolf.

In the struggle against religious persecution, as in the struggle against all evil, two struggles are always going on. One struggle is against the evil of persecution. This struggle must be fought relentlessly. Hence I am still in favor of sanctions when other nonviolent measures prove fruitless. The other struggle is against the evil in the soul of the one who struggles against the evil in the world.

Writing just after World War II, C. G. Jung said: "It is a fact that cannot be denied: the wickedness of others becomes our own wickedness because it kindles something evil in our own hearts." As we think of the persecuted Christians or any other persecuted group, we need to pray not only for them but also for ourselves — for the courage to defend them and for innocence as we do so.

In My Own Voice?

"We would like to have you speak in your own voice about what you believe as a Jew or Christian," wrote the editors inviting me to contribute to a volume in which Jews and Christians were to engage each other's traditions. I accepted the invitation, but the more I thought about "in your own voice," the more ambivalent I felt about it. I knew, of course, what the editors meant. I should not write as though I were not involved, as though I did not identify with my tradition. Instead of bracketing my own religious commitments and perspectives by using a descriptive and distancing mode of discourse, I should let these commitments and perspectives come to the surface and let the reader see where and how the tradition has a claim on me.

All this was fine with me — a theologian who believes that his calling is also to be a witness. And yet I felt uneasy. I was troubled about how my own voice would be heard in the contemporary climate, which places a high premium on "authentic," "unique," and "properly one's own" experiences and views. With my own voice in the foreground, people would be more likely to stay with the text, of course. But would they not get the wrong impression about the character of the Christian faith? Might I not be suggesting to them that the Christian faith is some private philosophy put together from a smorgasbord of traditionally inherited or contextually available beliefs and practices, so as to suit a person's affinities and needs? Which, of course, it is not.

In Christianity, as in other major religions, the content of one's faith is primarily something one receives rather than something one puts together or creates. When a Christian says, "I believe," he or she always means, "I *too* believe" — I believe what the prophets and the apostles believed, I believe what the community of faith believed through the centuries. They believed, and together with them I too believe. What I believe as myself, a person living in a particular time and place, is important. But at its heart, that should be nothing but a personally and situationally appropriate variation of what others have believed and what I have received.

In his comments about what Jesus Christ means to him, the great Protestant theologian of the last century, Karl Barth, expressed the idea with his usual rhetorical flourish:

> If I were to single out something special that he is for me, I should be missing what in fact he is specifically for me. He is for me in particular precisely what before me, outside me and alongside me, he is for all Christians and indeed for the whole world and for all men. He is this specifically for me too.

If this were understood, I thought, I could speak in my own voice. Indeed, as a believer living here and now, I must do so. Speaking in my own voice would be letting the "received" shine through what is "my own" and offering "my own" as a particular case of the "received." But would this be understood by readers?

Beliefs in living religions are characterized by a peculiar interrelation of "received" and "one's own." Paying heed to that interrelation is especially important in interreligious exchanges. But widespread cultural sensibilities want things differently. When representatives of religions disagree, people today increasingly expect of them what they expect of their politicians — a negotiated settlement. The one side needs to give up a bit here and the other side a bit there, and, barring some culpable stubbornness on one or both sides, we should arrive at a happy compromise.

If religious beliefs were privately constructed "life philosophies" that satisfied an individual's or community's private needs and desires, such an expectation would be reasonable. But if religious beliefs, in addition to whatever else they may be, are received deposits of faith with a claim to truth, then it is not at our discretion to give up — or take over — a bit of them here and there.

Interreligious exchanges should be very unlike political negotiations. Instead of aiming at pragmatic compromises that suit our own idiosyncratic needs and wishes, we must embark upon a much more interesting and profitable venture of reading others' beliefs and practices through the lenses of our own tradition and examining how our own beliefs and practices are read by others and why. It will be a venture of trying to make sense of other traditions on their own terms as well as from our perspective, and of noting their responses to our beliefs and practices. We will inquire what light such process sheds on our own tradition and on how it can be clarified, purified, and enriched, or even — God forbid! — given up.

We must engage religious beliefs not in isolation, but as elements of traditions — dynamic and evolving traditions maybe, but traditions nonetheless. So I wrote about what I *too* believe. Did doing so in any way entail a diminution of my own "authenticity"? Certainly not. For I wrote about the faith which came to me in such a way as to become so much my own that it formed the very self who was now, quite cheerfully, writing in "his own voice" about what he had received.

Be Particular

At an interfaith conference in Skopje, Macedonia, I began a keynote address with a few remarks on what it means to speak in a Christian voice in an interfaith setting. Since religious pluralism increasingly defines the American social landscape and since religions are an important factor in the way we relate to each other, it is important for us to reflect on this issue.

Some suggest that all major world religions are at bottom more or less the same. What is significant in each is common to them all. What makes each differ from others is only a husk conditioned by various human mentalities but holding an identical kernel. In *An Interpretation of Religion,* John Hick comes close to this view in arguing that, in the words of Muslim mystic Jalalu'l-Din Rumi, "the lamps are different, but the Light is the same." To speak in a Christian voice from the perspective of such an understanding of religion means to engage in cracking the husk of difference that distinguishes the Christian faith from other religions and displaying the kernel that unites it with them. Whoever speaks authentically in a Christian voice will end up agreeing with representatives of other religions provided they do the same.

While I think that major religions have much in common, including some fundamental convictions, and that their adherents all possess the same human dignity and therefore command the same respect, I disagree with Hick. It is not clear that all religions are essentially the same. Most of their adherents would disagree with the claim, and would feel that the one making it does not sufficiently respect them in their own specificity but is looking through them in search of an artificially constructed "essence" of what they are about.

My sense is that practitioners of religions are right in this regard. Major religions represent distinctive overarching interpretations of life with partly overlapping and partly competing metaphysical, historical, and moral claims. To treat all religions as at bottom the same is to insert them into a frame of meaning without sufficiently appreciating, as Michael Barnes puts it in *Theology and the Dialogue of Religions,* "the irreducible mystery of otherness" of religions. It is because all major religions are not in essence the same that engaging in dialogues is worthwhile; such dialogues are exercises in deep mutual learning about ourselves and others. Equally, it is because all major religions are not at the bottom the same that their adherents rightly argue with each other about the merits and truth content of their respective religions.

An alternative view claims not only that major world religions represent distinct, overarching interpretations of life, but also that the important points of each tradition lie precisely in the places where they differ. This view is rarely defended theoretically, and it represents more of an unreflective way of relating to other religions, a stance toward them. With such a stance, what matters the most, for instance, is not that the children of Abraham all believe in one God, but that Christians believe that this one God is a Holy Trinity, whereas Jews and Muslims staunchly object to this claim. To speak in a Christian voice is to highlight what is specific to Christianity and leave out what is common as comparatively unimportant.

But concentrating on differences seems to be a major mistake and includes a misconception about the proper way to define something. As any introduction to logic will make clear, you cannot define an entity by noting only its specific difference; you must also include in your definition its proximate genus. Human beings are rational animals; "rational" is the specific difference and "animal" is the proximate genus, and the one does not exist in a human being without the other. Applied to the world of religions, what is important about the Christian convictions about God is not simply that God is the Holy Trinity, but also that the Father of Jesus Christ is the God who called Abraham and delivered the Jews from slavery in Egypt, who is, from a Christian perspective, the God whom Muslims worship as Allah. Similarly, what is important about the Christian sacred texts is not only that they contain the New Testament, but also that they contain what Christians call the Old Testament, which is originally a Jewish sacred text, and that there is a significant overlap between Christian and Muslim sacred texts. To think of one's own or of another religion simply in terms of its differences from one's own is to fail to respect it in its concreteness.

In fact, both of the above approaches are wrongheaded because they abstract from the concrete character of religions, one by zeroing in on what is the same in all religions and the other by zeroing in on what is different. In this they miss precisely what is most important about a religion — the particular configuration of its elements, which may overlap with, differ from, or contradict elements of other religions. Religions are embraced and practiced in no other way except in their concreteness. To speak in a Christian voice is neither to give a variation on a theme common to all religions nor to make exclusively Christian claims in distinction from all other religions. It is to give voice to the Christian faith in its concreteness, whether what is said overlaps with, differs from, or contradicts what people speaking in a Jewish or Muslim voice are saying. Since truth matters, and since a false pluralism of approving pats on the back is cheap and short-lived, we will rejoice over overlaps and engage others over differences and incompatibilities, so as both to learn from and teach others.

Your Scripture Meets Mine

A few months ago, I participated in a Building Bridges Seminar, one of the annual encounters between Muslim and Christian theologians sponsored by Lambeth Palace. I was not quite sure what to expect going in. Such dialogues can range from boring to exhilarating. They are boring when both parties repeat predictable lines; they are exhilarating when each, without betraying its own identity, opens itself up to the adventure of encounter with the other. The dialogue in which I took part was exhilarating, and the main reason was the method. It was organized around reading our holy scriptures together, one session a text from the Bible and the next session a text from the Qur'an, and so on. There are two advantages to engaging one another by reading scriptures together.

First, it brings movement to calcified positions. We might reasonably fear that appealing to scripture could close off further discussion. After all, a community's scripture is its final authority. By appealing to it, interlocutors could easily come to the point where they say to each other, "Our scripture says this and your scripture says that, and that's that!" and be off to the next subject or, more distressingly, go their separate ways to not only disagree but to fight. Some would say that instead of discussing scriptural texts, it might be better to discuss our communally significant convictions and practices.

But if we take away the scripture, we have little to say when, after prolonged and strenuous disagreement, our interlocutors tell us, "This is what we think; this is what we do" — except accusing them of being either irrational or irresponsible or pointing out that we are simply different. Put the scripture at the center of the dialogue, and deadlock can be avoided. The disputes are now less about us and our opinions and more about something that has a claim on us and to which we give greater allegiance than we do to our own convictions.

A report from a previous session of the Building Bridges Seminar was titled *Scripture in Dialogue.* If we put scripture at the center of the dialogue, we become not so much agents of a dialogue as instruments of a dialogue whose main protagonists are our respective scriptures. Put differently, the dialogue is then not primarily about us; or rather, it is about us only because it is about our scripture. As long as we hold on to the scripture, we can loosen the grip with which we hold on to our own convictions. We are firmly rooted and yet open to change.

For introducing movement to calcified positions, almost as important as the authority of the scriptures is their immense richness. They are like the surface of the ocean, always the same and yet always changing, depending on the light, the wind, and the tides. Or, if one prefers a more solid metaphor, they are like mountain peaks, solid and immovable and yet always changing as the seasons change, as the sun falls on them from different angles, or as we circle around them. Such inexhaustibility of the scriptures is a further reason why the dialogue around them can be so fruitful. Given both the authority and the complexity of scripture, a rich and continuing discussion can ensue with the potential to change both parties without threatening their identities as people of this or that holy book.

The second advantage of the scripture-in-dialogue method is related to the way that we have used our scriptures. In the past, for example, Christians and Muslims have justified and made war against each other using scripture. We often engaged in interpretive endeavors as self-enclosed communities at odds with one another; we interpreted scripture not just to bolster our own identity in the face of the other but also to put down the other, even to harm the other.

As a Christian, I have come to consider such interpretations of scripture sinful, even when they turn out to be formally correct. At the heart of the Christian faith lies a claim that, out of incomprehensible love, our Lord Jesus Christ died for us while we were still God's enemies, and therefore, as those who are called to imitate Christ, we can and must love all people, even our enemies. When we engage other communities, whether of friends or enemies, such love demands that we try to see them as they see themselves and to see ourselves as they see us.

Given that we are people of the book, such love demands that we listen to how others perceive us as readers of our scripture as well as enter sympathetically into their efforts to interpret their scripture. In other words, we are called to practice interpretive hospitality — to visit each other's homes and to exchange gifts as we do so. Such hospitality will not necessarily lead to agreement in the interpretation of our respective scriptures. And it will likely not lead to wholesale agreement between our communities, for the simple reason that we hold very distinct — even if overlapping — texts as authoritative. But such interpretive hospitality will help us better understand our own and others' scripture, and discourage us from interpreting them in opposition to each other.

To practice such hospitable readings of each other's scripture, we do not have to consider them as somehow on the same footing, both identical with God's revelation. We may well consider the scripture of our interlocutors as a revisable prophetic word of God or indeed as nothing more than a powerful and influential human word. Yet even with such stances — stances that a majority of Christians and Muslims espouse — it is possible and fruitful to practice the hospitable reading of each other's holy books.

I went away from the Building Bridges Seminar with a renewed conviction that in interfaith dialogues — indeed, in all the disputes in which we Christians engage — a wise strategy is to go back to the scripture, together.

CULTURE AND POLITICS

Allegiance and Rebellion

I t was Good Friday 1997. There I was in the Los Angeles Convention Center with five thousand other people hailing from every nation on the face of the earth. No, it was not a multinational gathering of Christians assembled to worship the Crucified One. We were there to be sworn in as citizens of the United States of America. On the day when Christians all over the world confess allegiance to Jesus Christ, I was to swear my allegiance to a political power. The thought that the state was seeking symbolically to supplant faith and insinuate itself in the place of the Master of the Universe crept into my consciousness, and I could not just dismiss it.

An urge came on me to rebel against the state in the very moment of becoming its citizen. I did rebel, in a sense. When the whole crowd recited the "Oath of Allegiance to the United States," I kept silent as the others declared that they would "bear arms on behalf of the United States when required by the law."

On my application for naturalization I stated that I would not bear arms. To demonstrate the sincerity of my convictions, I appended a brief statement explaining that in communist Yugoslavia I had been persecuted partly because of my pacifist stance. The explanation didn't help. To be exempt from the obligation to bear arms in the United States, I had to be a member of a recognized religious body with an official pacifist position.

During an interview about my application for citizenship, my interlocutor tried to persuade me to change my mind.

"A stapler is an 'arm,'" said the exasperated woman behind the counter.

"I use a stapler every day," I responded, "but not to kill people."

"We don't want you to kill people!"

"So we agree?"

"But would you not defend your wife and your children?"

"I will defend, but I will not kill."

"There are mean people out there, ruthless autocrats, you know."

"Yes I know. I was born in the former Yugoslavia."

"Then you should know better."

"Maybe I do," I said.

Later, another official listened for about ten minutes to my dozen ways of saying "I will defend, but not bear arms" and then suggested a compromise. At the place on the form where I had checked that I will not bear arms, she drew a line and wrote, "Will defend." I initialed, and was granted permission to become a citizen — citizen Volf, who will defend without bearing arms . . . except staplers, of course.

It is not precisely accurate to say it was rebellion that occupied the forefront of my mind during the ceremony. But there was a struggle going on inside of me during the whole of it.

I had taken along an issue of *Christian Century* to read during my unoccupied moments. It contained a review of Jimmy Carter's *Living Faith*. I read about a recent president who asserted that Christian faith "has always been at the core of my existence"; a public servant whose attempts to unite spirituality and social service were shaped profoundly by Koinonia Farms and Habitat for Humanity, particularly "by their concern for racial reconciliation and for alleviating poverty"; a politician who has done door-to-door evangelism with an Hispanic pastor.

None of this was conceivable for a politician in the world I came from. I grew up under the totalitarian rule of communists whose declared goal was to stamp out the Christian faith, if not today, then tomorrow. Along with many others, I was beaten up and jailed for the simple act of publicly proclaiming the gospel. Later the communists were replaced by democratically elected nationalists. There was a marked difference between them, but mainly in style, not substance. The politicians carefully nurtured the image of being good and loyal members of the church — as a weapon in political battles and as a screen for blatant disregard of Christian precepts about personal integrity and social justice.

What would it take for a person the likes of Jimmy Carter to be elected as president of my native and still beloved Croatia?

My question was not born of naïvete. I am sufficiently suspicious of political power that I'd want to peek behind Carter's words and look at the record. And I know that because national politics did not mix well with prophetic activism, he was not reelected. Yet his Christian moral vision and pattern of social engagement remain rare among "Christian" politicians. And if it is true that democracies get the leaders they deserve, then for all its wrongs there is something profoundly right about the nation that would choose him as its president. I was happy to be a citizen of such a country.

A day or so after I was naturalized, I received a congratulatory card from my in-laws. It featured not a patriotic slogan but this quotation:

> As citizens, Christians share all things with others, and yet endure all things as if foreigners. Every foreign land is to them as their native country, and every land of their birth as a land of strangers. . . . They pass their days on earth, but they are citizens of heaven. They obey the prescribed laws, and at the same time surpass the laws by their lives.

The passage was from the early second-century *Epistle of Mathetus to Diognetus.* The words put in a memorable way the dialectic of distance and belonging, of strangeness and domesticity, of surpassing the laws and obeying them. A word of welcome appropriate to citizen Volf, who for the first time would be celebrating Independence Day as an American citizen — a citizen whose ultimate allegiance is to a polity ruled by the crucified Messiah.

Jesus — Left Behind

I am angry, and here is why.

A few months ago a friend told me of a conversation he'd had with an atheist in Colorado Springs. If you think that Colorado Springs, the Mecca of American evangelical Christianity, is the last place an atheist would feel at home, you are probably right. But there he was living, right in the middle of what from his perspective must have felt like a lion's den. My friend had met him and started talking to him about Jesus. The man was interested. Even those who, on facing Christians, feel like a piece of meat thrown before hungry beasts are often attracted to Jesus. After the men had studied the Gospels for a few weeks, the atheist's fascination with Jesus grew, but he was puzzled about his spiritual guide. "What kind of Christian are you?" he inquired of my friend. "If you really want to slap a label on me, it should probably read 'Evangelical.'" "You can't be an evangelical," responded his interlocutor, even more puzzled. "You are talking about Jesus!"

The story had a force of revelation for me. Evangelicals who belong to the religious right insist that Jesus is their Lord and savior, but nowadays many of them hardly ever talk about Jesus, at least not in public. They talk about politics — how to get their people elected to local, state, and federal governments so as to advance their religious, moral, and political causes. They pour all their energy into political battles, with none left for Jesus. If you were to point this out to them, they'd vehemently disagree by telling you that they wage political wars for Jesus and in his name. But Jesus is no longer at the center of their attention. The struggle for power has taken his place. They are political warriors in religious garb, not followers of Jesus. It took a religious outsider to name what was going on among the seemingly most devout.

There are many ways of leaving Jesus behind. Take the famous *Left Behind* series. Jesus is all over these books. But what kind of Jesus? As I was flipping through the pages of the series, I felt more in the world of Terminator movies than in the world of the Gospels or even the world of the book of Revelation. Violent struggle dominates the imagination of the writers, struggle carried out with most deadly weapons of the flesh. Jesus who came to redeem the world by the power of his self-giving love and who demanded of his would-be followers to take up their crosses and walk in his footsteps is nowhere to be seen. Overcoming the assaults of the godless enemy by the power of sacrificial witness to the point of shedding one's own blood!? The martyrs of the ancient book of Revelation have morphed into *Left Behind*'s ruthless warriors. And where is Jesus in all this? He is there, but not as the One who loves enemies and justifies the ungodly. That Jesus has been wholly subsumed by the Rider on the White Horse. Never mind that the whole of the New Testament is united in this crucial point: to follow Christ means to love one's enemies, not to eliminate them.

I am not sure which is worse: trading Jesus for political warring, or transmuting him into the image of our own violent selves. In a sense, though, both amount to the same: either way, Jesus is left behind.

Think of the irony involved. The religious *right* is abandoning Jesus! The charge that the religious left has abandoned Jesus for their pet political causes has been the religious right's standard line of attack against their religious enemies for quite some time. That charge isn't unjustified, of course. You need not belong to the religious right to notice a consistent pattern in the ways many theological liberals have thought about Jesus: Out with the Jesus of the Gospels and in with the "historically reconstructed" Jesus — which is to say, out with the Jesus who is a "stranger" to us and can challenge contemporary prejudices and in with the Jesus who is cast into our own image and fits with what is politically attractive or expedient. It does not seem to help to point this danger out, as many have done. You like what you like, and if you are at liberty to construe Jesus — which is what much of the reconstruction of the "historical" Jesus amounts to — you'll construe him to your liking.

Or instead of reconstructing Jesus, many on the religious left have chosen to disregard him. I've sat through many a sermon about this or that cause, this or that social or psychic technique for solving problems, if only we will roll up our sleeves and get to work. It is not that I dislike causes on the whole, but I keep wondering, Where is Jesus in all this? At best I can hear distant echoes of the "spirit" of Jesus translated into a modern idiom. Social causes, not the concrete person Jesus, have captured imagination.

Complaints that the religious left has abandoned Jesus are not new. And now the religious right has fashioned itself in the inverted image of the religious left. If this analysis is even roughly correct, the writing on the wall is spelling the doom of the religious right. Just think, the *political* power of the religious right is parasitic on its *religious* power, and its *religious* power is the direct result of the erstwhile centrality of *Jesus* in the life of its communities. Discard Jesus and you've not only foolishly replaced the one true God with idols of your own making — you've also cut off the branch that holds you up as a political player.

The challenge for the religious right *and* left who want to think of themselves as Christian is to show that Jesus matters more than politics. Then, and only then, will both be true leaven in the world of politics.

Shopkeeper's Gold

"I am walking the streets that are dead," sang Bob Dylan. As I heard the line, I remembered my own walk through streets that were dead. A year ago I visited Vukovar, a Croatian city that was virtually destroyed during a recent war. I saw emptiness gaping through the broken windows, and doors of houses whose roofs had caved in and whose facades bore scars of shrapnel. I heard the shrill silence that enveloped long rows of houses separated by pavement overgrown with weeds and littered with abandoned objects. Dead streets. Monuments of life destroyed or driven out.

More recently I walked the dead streets of Sandtown in inner-city Baltimore. It was as though I were reliving Vukovar, only this time the destroyer was not war but racial tensions, crime, and economic ruin. There was another important difference. Twelve blocks of the city had been carved out by New Song Community and designated as the space of God's peace. Dead streets newly infused with life.

Mark Gornik of New Song made the point almost in passing. As he was explaining the blight of the inner cities, he suggested that the doctrine of justification by grace contains untapped resources for healing. He should know, I thought. For some ten years he had been living and working in Sandtown and seen transformation taking place, one house at a time.

Yet for many a theologian, justification by grace is an idle doctrine. Some have abandoned it and left it to rust away on a theological junk heap; they deem it generally useless or at least unhelpful when it comes to healing even lesser social pathologies than cycles of poverty, violence, and hopelessness. Others pursue a kind of antiquarian interest in the doctrine; they examine and polish an artifact from the sixteenth century and pridefully show it to whoever may frequent their little museum. Whether rusty or polished, the doctrine of justification by grace lies there uninhabited, lifeless. A dead doctrine.

Could the hope for inner cities lie in part in the retrieval of the doctrine of justification by grace? How could dead streets receive life from a dead doctrine? Imagine that you have no job, no money, you live cut off from the rest of society in a world ruled by poverty and violence, your skin is the "wrong" color — and you have no hope that any of this will change.

Around you is a society governed by the iron law of achievement. Its gilded goods are flaunted before your eyes on TV screens, and in a thousand ways society tells you every day that you are worthless because you have no achievements. You are a failure, and you know that you will continue to be a failure because there is no way to achieve tomorrow what you have not managed to achieve today. Your dignity is shattered and your soul is enveloped in the darkness of despair.

But the gospel tells you that you are not defined by outside forces. It tells you that you count — even more, that you are loved unconditionally and infinitely, irrespective of anything you have achieved or failed to achieve, even that you are loved a tad bit more than those whose efforts have been crowned with success.

Imagine now this gospel not simply proclaimed but embodied in a community that has emerged not as a "result of works" but as a community "created in Christ Jesus for good works" (Eph. 2:10). Justified by sheer grace, it seeks to "justify" by grace those who are made "unjust" by society's implacable law of achievement. Imagine furthermore this community determined to infuse the wider culture, along with its political and economic institutions, with the message that it seeks to embody and proclaim. This is justification by grace, proclaimed and practiced. A dead doctrine? Hardly.

As I was reflecting on the social significance of justification by grace, I remembered a passage from Nietzsche's *Thus Spoke Zarathustra* that I had read on the way to Baltimore. "O my brothers, I direct and consecrate you to a new nobility: you shall become begetters and cultivators and sowers of the future — truly, not a nobility that you could buy like shopkeepers with shopkeepers' gold: for all that has a price is of little value."

Justification by grace, I thought, musing on Nietzsche's profound observation, is so deeply at odds with our "shopkeepers' culture." It takes the price tags off human beings not so as to devalue them but so as to give them their proper dignity, a dignity not based on what they have achieved but rooted in the sheer fact that they are loved unconditionally by God. Divine love is that indispensable nourishment for the human soul of which the prophet speaks when he calls, "Ho, everyone who thirsts, come to the waters; and you that have no money, come, buy and eat! Come, buy wine and milk without money and without price" (Isa. 55:1).

Floating Along?

It was with a dose of suspicion that I started reading the feature article in the *New York Times Magazine* (February 27, 2000) about the Schreibners, a large family intent on creating a well-defined Christian subculture in the midst of what, from its perspective, is a world gone hopelessly awry. The parents shop at consignment stores, homeschool their kids, keep the teen pop culture at bay (no Leonardo DiCaprio posters!), and teach traditional family values. I have tended to think of such people as well-intentioned but naïve folk who believe they can replicate for themselves the world of their pious grandparents. Which is my definition of fundamentalism.

I knew, however, that my tendency had done the family an injustice when I read the following sentence in Margaret Talbot's article. The "way they practice their faith," she writes, "puts them so sharply and purposefully at odds with the larger culture that it is hard not to see the Schreibners, conservative and law-abiding though they are, as rebels." Two further paragraphs in the article set this strange rebelliousness in context:

> We have arrived, it seems, at a moment in our history when the most vigorous and coherent counterculture around is the one constructed by conservative Christians. That sounds odd to many of us — especially, perhaps, to secular liberals, who cherish our own '60s-inflected notions of what an "alternative lifestyle" should look like. Ever since Theodore Roszak first coined it in 1968, the word "counterculture" has retained its whiff of patchouli, its association with free love, long hair and left-wing youth.

Yet today it is conservative Christians like the Schreibners who, more self-consciously than any other large social group, buck the mainstream notions of what constitutes a fulfilled life. Indeed, much of what Roszak said of the '60s counterculture could be said of them too. It's true that the "patterns" and "mores" they have discovered are not so much new ones as reinvigorated traditional ones. Parent-sanctioned courtship, the merging of school and home, the rejection of peer-group segregation, the moral value of thrift all are ideas that, in the United States, last held real sway in the 19th century. But the impatience that people like the Schreibners display with acquisition, their unflagging commitment to putting the group — in their case, the family — above individual ambition, their rejection of pop culture . . . make them radical in ways that would be recognizable to some '60s counter-culturalists too.

For some time now I have been troubled by the seeming disappearance of any robust alternative to the pervasive culture of late capitalism, whether in the church or in the society at large. We are drowning in a flood of consumer goods and are drenched in showers of media images. We live in a smorgasbord culture in which everything is interesting and nothing really matters. We have lost a vision of the good life, and our hopes for the future are emptied of moral content. Instead of purposefully walking to determinate places, we are aimlessly floating with random currents. Of course, we do get exercised by issues and engage in bitter feuds over them. But that makes us even less capable of resisting the pull of the larger culture, a resistance that would take shape in formulating and embodying a coherent alternative way of life.

The Schreibners have done what the rest of us seem incapable of doing: they have created an alternative culture. And they have done so in the only way that is responsible — namely, by being "selective separatists." They vote, pay taxes, work in the mainstream world (Mr. Schreibner is an American Airlines pilot), even do community service; but they also deliberately choose, as Mrs. Schreibner puts it, "not to participate in those parts of the culture that do not bring glory to God." One can disagree with some aspects of the alternative culture that the Schreibners have chosen to create. I am not so sure, for instance, that a father must be the breadwinner in the family and that a mother's only place is at home with the children. But instead of complaining about the particulars of a robust fundamentalist counterculture, we should ask ourselves: Why are *we* seemingly incapable of creating a viable and vibrant alternative?

The inability of many Christians today to live out a coherent set of practices in selective separation from the larger culture also has a cognitive side. If we are neither fundamentalists nor evangelicals, we find it difficult to formulate clearly and bindingly the content of the gospel. Some time ago, *Christianity Today* offered a summary of the gospel titled "The Gospel of Jesus Christ: An Evangelical Celebration." It was signed by a broad spectrum of fundamentalist and evangelical leaders. With few exceptions, mainline reactions to the document were negative. Commentators found the definition of the gospel too narrow and the document as a whole lacking in theological depth. But could they agree on a more adequate formulation of what is at the heart of the gospel? Mainline churches seem incapable of producing such an alternative — for the same reason, I suspect, that they are incapable of generating a set of robust countercultural practices.

If we can neither state what the gospel is, nor have a clear notion of what constitutes the good life, we will more or less simply float along, like jellyfish with the tide. True, a belief in our ability to shape the wider culture is woven into the fabric of our identity. So we complain and we act. But in the absence of determinate beliefs and practices, our criticism and activism will be little more than one more way of floating along.

Rules, Rules, and More Rules

It may seem odd that at the beginning of the twenty-first century our lives are so pervasively dominated by rules, big rules and small rules, rules that frame our interactions and rules that enter into the fine fabric of our personal lives. After all, at least since the Enlightenment the epochal trend has been to carve out more space for the individual's freedom — freedom from the church, from God, from the state, from conventional morality, from nosy neighbors. Freedom to craft ourselves into whatever shape we deem fitting. In short, freedom from everything and everybody and freedom for anything. But freedom of this sort comes at a price. And the price is, paradoxically, entanglement in a thick web of rules and regulations.

In an essay titled "In Lieu of Manners," Jeffrey Rosen notes that following the dismantling of traditional hierarchies, "the vocabulary of law and legalisms is the only shared language we have left for regulating behavior in an era in which there is no longer a social consensus about how men and women, and even boys and girls, should behave." He describes the phenomenon as "an explosion of legalisms." This explosion of legalisms is different from and much more pervasive than the commonly bemoaned "explosion of litigation." Most of us, Rosen notes, will never be parties in an actual court case. But all of us are experiencing the increasing regulation of our lives by "rules and laws" instead of "manners and mores."

What's so bad, comparatively speaking, about "rules and laws"? "Manners and mores" can be just as oppressive and can carry a false aura of inevitability, while rules and laws are just what they are — changing codes by which people regulate their common life. We might decide that our "rules" serve us better than "manners." And we might prefer either of them to "God's laws."

For with God's laws, life is regulated by something unbending and unchangeable, with an authority derived from the sacred and absolute. Though we might not like most human "rules and laws," we might like the idea of a divine lawgiver and divine laws even less. Without God we are freer, because we live by our rules and our laws, not by laws imposed on us from above. Such reasoning is pleasing to the ears of freedom-loving inhabitants of modernity. But is it persuasive?

Consider what happens if we don't like a particular rule. We can go to court and challenge it. But what if we don't like the decision of the court? We go to the Supreme Court. There's no guarantee, though, that we'll like the ruling of the Supreme Court either. Rightly or wrongly, that court's *Bush v. Gore* ruling struck many liberals and moderates as ideological and partisan. Cynicism in relation to the rulings of the Supreme Court lands us in dire straits if all we have are "rules and laws." We must *have* them to regulate our common life, but in the absence of anyone with uncontested moral authority, there's nobody to make the rules really stick — and hence they seem arbitrary. As a result, we are less and less effective in dealing with social tensions. For that purpose, God's laws have a distinct advantage over human regulations. As long as they are affirmed *as* God's laws, it is hard to be cynical about them. People might not *like* them, but what are people's likes and dislikes compared to the excellence of God's character, the weight of divine authority?

So far, the argument in favor of God's laws may not satisfy fully. It does not satisfy me because it is way too pragmatic for my taste. So here is an important addition: "Rules and laws" regulate the formalities of our interactions; they are not a reflection of who, in a deep sense, we as human beings are. They are external to our being; they are a means to our getting along with one another.

It is different with the divine laws. These are an expression of the divine being, and they map what it means to live human lives well. When we live in accordance with divine laws, we are fulfilling our calling as human beings. In holy scripture, people are said to "delight" in God's law, whereas it would be strange to say that a person delights in "rules and regulations." Rules and regulations are a necessary evil; God's law is a positive good. This "goodness" of the divine law explains the trajectory we find in the scriptures' understanding of how God's law is related to human beings. In the Old Testament, the law of Moses was given to the people on tablets of stone. In the New Testament, the law of the Messiah is written on "hearts of flesh." In the world to come, God's law will become so much a part of ourselves that the only thing we will ever want is to do what it commands.

You may think that next I'm going to recommend that we place the Ten Commandments in all our courtrooms, return prayer to our schools, and impose divine law throughout the land. Have I not argued that an uncontestable authority such as God's may have some social advantages over changing human rules? Have I not maintained that God's laws are an expression of who we are called to be? Yet I think that all such recommendations about the public role of religion are mistaken. We no longer live in the pious world of our Puritan foreparents. And I am not sure that it was right even then to impose divine law on the nation, much less now that we live in an irreversibly pluralist society.

There is an alternative both to being constricted by human rules and to having divine laws imposed on us. If we want freedom — freedom from rules, freedom to be our best self, freedom to enjoy both God and neighbor — then we will seek to have God's laws inscribed on our hearts. Everything else is slavery, more or less!

Nothing but the Truth

We often engage in disputes about how events from the past should be remembered. Whether we've had an argument with a child, a quarrel with a spouse, or a debate about national history, the truth about the past seems to matter a great deal. And yet there are powerful voices in our culture that tell us we should let go of this interest. The truth about the past cannot be had, the argument goes, and the demand for truth is dangerous. I disagree strenuously. I believe that we have a moral obligation to remember truthfully.

Suppose I were skiing at Mammoth Mountain in California with my friend Alexander. One evening, with Alexander present, I say to my friends, "Today we went up chair twenty-six to the top of the mountain and skied down Drop Out." Alexander looks at me and says, "No, no, no! We turned right and skied down Wipe Out." The mistake is innocent; it is just a matter of remembering the name of the run or the direction in which we turned at the top of the mountain. If I'm telling what happened, though, I have an obligation to tell it truthfully. Of course I could also and legitimately tell a fictional story, or engage in the creative renarration of events designed to elicit laughter or make a point. And in those cases the obligation of truth-telling does not apply in the same way. As Paul Ricoeur argues in *The Reality of the Historical Past,* "When one wants to indicate the difference between fiction and history one unavoidably invokes the idea of a certain correspondence between the narrative and what really happened." True, correspondence is always a reconstruction — "a different construction than the course of events reported." But the narrator's relation to the past is that of an "unpaid debt," argues Ricoeur. "This idea of debt, which may seem strange at first, appears to me to emerge out of an expression common to the painter and to the historian: both seek to 'render' a landscape, a course of events. Under the term 'render' can be recognized the intention of 'rendering its due to what is and to what was.'"

The obligation to truthfulness is heightened if a story reflects well or badly on a person's character. Imagine if I told my skiing story like this: "From the top of the chair lift, we started skiing toward Drop Out; Alexander was a bit shaky when he looked at the sheer vertical drop, but I went straight down with no problem." In this case Alexander might have replied, "Wait a second. You chickened out! You wanted to ski all the way around the back of the mountain; *I* was the one who went down first!" Alexander's intervention here is more significant than in the previous case. In the way I was remembering and retelling what happened, I was unjustly bolstering my reputation and undermining his. It matters whether I skied down Drop Out, or who skied down it first, because the memory entails comparative judgments about me in relation to Alexander. Hence I have a moral obligation to remember truthfully. In such cases, to remember untruthfully is to act unjustly. This is even truer in cases that involve conflict between parties. At bottom, the obligation to truthfulness is an obligation to justice.

What about possible dangers associated with this obligation? If both parties claim to know the truth of what transpired between them, but their "truths" clash, they will have all the more reason to cross swords. This caveat seems right on the whole, although one can very well imagine that even in a conflict situation a person can stick to her version of the story as true but eschew any form of violence and refuse to cross swords. I take this to be what the Christian faith demands of us all.

Notice, however, that the objection concerns the claim of each party to *possess* the truth, not the moral obligation of both to *seek* the truth. The clash is caused less by the fact that truthfulness matters to persons too much than by the fact that it matters too little — so little that they, as fallible human beings, can simply assert that they already possess the truth and therefore forgo seeking it. The claim to possess the truth may be dangerous when it matters to a person more than the truth itself. But this takes us back to the moral obligation to remember truthfully. A sense of obligation to remember truthfully will work against these dangers.

A moral obligation to truthfulness is salutary. If it is dangerous to give up the quest for truth out of claims already to possess it, it is also dangerous to give up the quest for truth out of satisfaction with multiple stories, none of them corresponding more to reality than the others. When Heinrich Himmler spoke to the SS troops in 1943, he lauded the project of the extermination of Jews as "a glorious page in our history which has *never been written and will never be written*" (italics added). With such attempts to hide the atrocities about to be committed in mind, historian Omar Bartov notes that efforts to come to terms with ambiguous reality by suggesting there are a multiplicity of equally valid perspectives "can play . . . easily into the hands of those who have no qualms about producing realities of the most horrific nature and then claiming that they had never taken place."

Giving up the moral obligation to remember truthfully is dangerous. Embracing this obligation is salutary — provided we don't subvert that obligation by false claims to possess the truth or by using those claims to justify violence.

Power Play

I n a lecture on the exercise of political power, David R. Young claimed
that although much attention is paid "to the physical and intellectual
dimensions" of the exercise of political power, little or none is paid today
to "the emotional, nonrational or spiritual dimension." And yet, argued
Young, "it is the spiritual character of the individual human being as a
whole . . . that has the greatest impact on how such power is wielded —
for better or worse, for good or ill." If Young is right — and I think he is —
then all will depend on how one understands spiritual character.

Consider Martin Luther and the Reformation he set in motion. True,
he was not a politician. He saw himself as a professor of the Holy Scriptures and a teacher of the church. Yet he set in motion epochal changes
in the culture and politics of sixteenth-century Europe, changes that
helped shape the history not only of Europe but also of the world. Leave
aside for a moment the debate about the merit of his accomplishments
— whether he was a God-sent prophet of true Christianity in an age of religious decadence (as Protestants liked to believe for centuries); a "sex-
crazed monk of furious temper, a liar and fraud willing to tumble down
the great and beautiful edifice of the Catholic Christianity for no better
motives than lust and pride" (as Catholics traditionally insisted); or a
revolutionary figure in the history of human freedom (as Hegel and Marx
thought), and whether, remembering especially the religious wars of the
seventeenth century, he brought more misery than well-being into the
world (as biographer Richard Marius argues). What is significant here is
to note the magnitude of events that depended on this one man.

In his book *Luther: An Introduction to His Thought,* Gerhard Ebeling comments on Luther's role in the dramatic events of the years 1517 to 1521:

> The real drama of these years consisted only in a secondary sense of impressive, tense and critical scenes such as the hearing before Cardinal Cajetan in Augsburg in 1518, the disputation in Leipzig with Johannes Eck in 1519, the burning of the bull of excommunication in 1520. . . . This course of events was not one which, once set in motion, continued automatically. Each further step depended to an astonishing degree upon the word of a single person, who had unintentionally presented a challenge to the contemporary world. If he had recanted at Augsburg, if he had been more cautious at Leipzig, if he had not rejected the judgment of the Pope, and if he had followed the advice of numerous well-intentioned friends and had been prepared to compromise, and if in some way he had come to an arrangement with the Imperial Diet, the course of the Reformation would have been different. . . . During these years, Luther's responsibility for the word of God resolved itself simply into clinging firmly to this word — something that was simple and straightforward in essence, but which represented for Luther, who stood alone and whose endurance was being tested, an ordeal by fire with a thousand trials and temptations, in a constantly changing situation.

Incredible as it may sound, Luther's word determined the course of history. But what made him cling to that word, all the religious and political pressures notwithstanding? Many explanations can be given, but ultimately we have to fall back on the mystery of his character. He became a reformer not because of his physical stamina or intellectual prowess, although these were formidable, but because of his character, because of his unique blend of emotional and spiritual traits.

As we think of Luther's influence, ultimately we cannot be concerned simply about the scale of his impact. We must assess its value. And it is here that the spiritual dimension in the exercise of political power becomes significant in a different and much more important sense. For spirituality can be merely a means of maintaining power and of better achieving political ends, whatever their moral content. Like

Machiavelli's prince, a politician will then strive to appear "to those who see him and hear him talk, all mercy, all faith, all integrity, all humanity, all religion." Or she will sincerely strive after such qualities but will apply them only to the limited circle of her family, friends, and political allies; she will act like a leader of a gang of robbers who is aware that her success depends on the loyalty, honesty, and self-sacrifice of its members. In contrast, if what ultimately matters is not naked political success but the well-being of a political community in the context of the larger world, then politicians must have not only spiritual character as individual human beings, but also character that is infused with a moral political vision.

Some years ago, I heard Alex Bourain of South Africa speak about Nelson Mandela's role in dismantling apartheid. He confirmed the importance of the single word of a single individual in critical situations. In delicate but hard negotiations with the apartheid regime, when things could have gone either way, it was often Mandela's demand to press on and not give up that made all the difference. The "word" dismantled apartheid because it was an outgrowth of the spiritual character of a person who was guided by a compelling moral vision.

Indefensible War

The "grave and gathering danger" hanging over the world is not so much the posited danger presented by Saddam Hussein as the danger of American preemptive war against Iraq. The current administration believes that such a war is necessary to remove Saddam Hussein from power, thus preventing him from acquiring nuclear capabilities and deploying them along with the biological and chemical weapons already in his possession. There is no doubt that Hussein's regime is evil, oppressive, and cruel toward its own citizenry, especially minorities, and that it represents a major threat to its near and distant neighbors. As Christians committed to justice and the well-being of all people, we must condemn Hussein's injustices and work toward a just government in Iraq. These same commitments should lead us, however, to condemn the proposed preemptive war.

Such a war is likely to bring long-term instability to a sensitive and volatile region and inflame Islamic extremism. It would violate standards of international law and create a dangerous precedent for other nations (China, India, Pakistan, Russia) leaning toward engaging in preemptive wars they believe are justified. Such political and legal considerations are reason enough not to start a war against Iraq. In addition, Christians must highlight compelling moral reasons against such a war and draw attention to the grave consequences it would have for already tense Christian-Muslim relations.

This essay was written prior to the start of the Iraq War.

Over the centuries Christians have developed two basic attitudes toward war. Both would rule out as immoral a preemptive war against Iraq. The first is pacifism, which opposes military action in all circumstances and thus condemns a preemptive war. From the perspective of this tradition, such war would be a perversion of Jesus' basic teachings and therefore not simply unchristian but positively anti-Christian. Whereas Jesus said, "If anyone strikes you on the right cheek, turn the other also," President Bush, who claims to be a follower of Jesus, says, "If you think that Hussein will strike you on one cheek, hit him, along with innocent bystanders."

According to the "just war" tradition, which does not deem all military action illegitimate, a preemptive war against Iraq would also be morally unacceptable. The central criterion is a "just cause." The Christian tradition has consistently understood that, in the words of Thomas Aquinas, "those who are attacked should be attacked because they deserve it on account of some fault." Preemptive war by definition does not satisfy this criterion, since it is waged not to "avenge wrongs" actually committed (Augustine), but to prevent wrongs that are only anticipated. Unless it were demonstrated that Hussein's regime posed a clearly identifiable and imminent danger to the United States (or to Iraq's neighbors), the war against Iraq would be manifestly unjust. No persuasive evidence of such a threat has yet been presented, and no links have been established between Hussein's regime and networks of terrorist organizations (except for a disputed and indirect report about Muhammed Atta meeting with an Iraqi intelligence agent in Prague).

A preemptive war is unjust for a very simple reason: it cannot be just to condemn masses of people to certain death in order to avert the potential death of an equal or lesser number of people. President Bush acts as though the entire population of Iraq consists of one single person. In his speech before the United Nations, he referred to the suffering of the Iraqi people — who oppose American intervention although they dislike their cruel leader — and cited this suffering as motivation for war. But he never mentioned the horrible deaths that would be an inescapable consequence of the war. The death toll among the Iraqi population in the planned war is likely to exceed the one hundred thousand Iraqi casualties of the 1991 Gulf War. This would pile suffering upon suffering, for

Iraqi people already groan, not only under the iron fist of their leader, but also under the sanctions imposed on Iraq after the Gulf War. According to United Nations statistics, five hundred thousand to one million Iraqi children have died as a consequence of sanctions. And we should not forget the likely American casualties, estimated by some at twenty to thirty thousand.

In addition to being indefensible on moral grounds, a preemptive war against Iraq would damage the already difficult relations between Christians and Muslims. In the popular Muslim perception, America is identified with Christianity. A war led by an American Christian president against a Muslim nation — even if most Muslim nations dislike that nation's regime — would be seen as a crusade against Islam. Daily pictures of suffering Iraqis in media throughout the Islamic world would fuel extremism and push young people into terrorist networks. Even more important (if one takes a long-term view of things), the war would make all efforts at reconciliation between Christianity and Islam extremely difficult. As a result, current efforts to bridge a gulf and lessen tensions between these two great traditions would be shut down.

The preemptive war against Iraq is not "a great moral cause and a great strategic goal," as President Bush claims. For political, legal, moral, and interfaith reasons, it is imperative for Christians to condemn the prospect of such a war unequivocally. Christians must organize demonstrations, the leaders of its churches must make public statements, and individuals must begin collecting signatures — all to prevent the leaders of our nation from engaging in an immoral and unwise war.

Guns and Crosses

Many intellectuals associate religion — and Christianity in particular — with violence. Hence they argue that the less religion we have the better off we will be. In an article in the *Atlantic Monthly,* for example, Jonathan Rauch argues that the greatest development in modern religion is "apatheism" — a sense of not caring one way or the other whether God exists. The best of all possible situations, says Rauch, is to be indifferent toward religion, whether you are religious or not.

Rauch is wrong. If we strip Christian convictions of their original and historic cognitive and moral content, and thereby reduce faith to a cultural resource endowed with a diffuse aura of the sacred, in situations of conflict, we are likely to get religiously legitimized and inspired violence. If, on the other hand, we nurture people in historic Christian convictions that are rooted in sacred texts, we will likely get militants for peace. This is a result of a careful examination of two things: the inner logic of Christian convictions and actual Christian practice.

In his book *The Ambivalence of the Sacred,* R. Scott Appleby argues on the basis of case studies that religious people play a positive role in the world of human conflicts and contribute to peace, not when they "moderate their religion or marginalize their deeply held, vividly symbolized and often highly particular beliefs," but rather "when they remain religious actors." Yet, like Rauch, many people think otherwise.

Even if this argument is sound (as I think it is), we still need to ask why misconceptions about the violent character of Christian faith abound. Part of the answer is that Christians have used and continue to use their faith to legitimize violence when they, for whatever reason, believe violence must be deployed. Misconceptions of the Christian faith mirror widespread misbehavior of Christians, and misbehavior of Christians goes hand in hand with misconstruing their own faith, and with "thinning" its original elements.

There is more. One can easily show that the majority of Christians — and the majority of religious folks in general — are nonviolent citizens, peace lovers, peacemakers, and even peace activists, not in spite of their religion but *for* religious reasons. The purveyors of violence who seek religious legitimization are statistically a small minority among Christians.

So why is the contrary opinion widespread? What Avishai Margalit writes about ethnic belonging applies equally well to religion: "It takes one cockroach found in your food to turn the otherwise delicious meal into a bad experience. . . . It takes 30 to 40 ethnic groups who are fighting one another to make the 1,500 or more significant ethnic groups in the world who live more or less peacefully look bad." One may describe this as "self-inflation of the negative," or the tendency of the evil to loom larger than the comparatively much more widely distributed good.

This tendency is strengthened in the modern world, where information flow is dominated by the mass media. Consider the following contrast: The Serbian paramilitary who rapes Muslim women with a cross around his neck has made it into the headlines and is immortalized in books on religious violence; but Katarina Kruhonja, a medical doctor from Osijek, Croatia, and a recipient of the alternative Nobel Prize for her peace initiatives, remains relatively unknown, as does the motivation for her work, which is thoroughly religious. While it's true that the success of people like Kruhonja depends on low visibility, our unawareness of it also has to do with the character of mass-media communication in a market-driven world. Violence sells, so viewers get to see violence.

The mass media create reality, but they do so by building on the proclivities of viewers. Why does the Serbian paramilitary rapist seem more "interesting" than Kruhonja? And why are we prone to conclude that his religious faith is implicated in the acts because he is wearing a cross, while it would never occur to us to blame the institution of marriage when we see a ring on his finger? Religion is more associated with violence than with peace in the public imagination partly because the public is fascinated with violence. We, the peace-loving citizens of nations whose tranquility is secured by effective policing, are insatiable observers of violence. And as voyeurs, we become vicarious participants in the very violence we outwardly abhor. We are particularly drawn to religious violence because we have a strong interest in exposing hypocrisy, especially of a religious kind. Put the two factors together — the inner deployment of violence and the delight in exposure — and it looks as though we want to hear about religious people's engagement in violence because *we* are violent but expect *them* to act otherwise.

If we were more self-critical about our violent proclivities and more suspicious about violence in the media, we might note, on the religious landscape, the steady flow of work that religious people do to make the world a more peaceful place. Our imagination would not be captured, for instance, with religion as the motivating force for a dozen or so not particularly religious terrorists who destroyed the Twin Towers. Instead, we would be impressed with the degree to which religion serves as a source of solace and orientation for a majority of Americans in a time of crisis. We'd note the motivation it gave to many to help the victims, protect Muslims from stereotyping by others, and build bridges between religious cultures. This kind of religion warrants our *promotion,* not indifference.

Terror in the Mind of God?

Not long after the 9/11 terrorist attack on the Twin Towers, in a class we read the text that catapulted Karl Barth to his theological fame: his *Epistle to the Romans,* written shortly after World War I. In the light of current events, what resonated with some of us most deeply was Barth's critique of religion. No, religion is not the solemn music that accompanies all the noblest human experiences, he argued. We see rather "sin celebrating its triumph in religion." Stung by his teachers' facile identifications of Western civilization with the "kingdom of God," Barth raged against religion: "Conflict and distress, sin and death, the devil and hell, make up the reality of religion." As I was reading these words last fall, I thought of the terrorist attackers and their religious inspiration in Islamic fundamentalism. What Barth had in mind, however, were not primarily *other* religions but his own — Christianity. World War I was an inner Christian affair.

While I resonated with Barth's critique of religion, I also felt a need to resist some of its contemporary appropriations. A sense that religions are irredeemably implicated in violence around the globe is prevalent among intellectuals and to a somewhat lesser degree in the general public. One can easily point to prominent examples of religion's fueling violence-inducing passions. Historically, the contemporary coupling of religion and violence feeds most decisively on memories of the wars that plagued Europe from the 1560s to the 1650s and raged around religious differences. Today also it seems that the gods have mainly terror on their minds — in Ireland, Serbia, and India, to name just a few sites in which religion has factored in bloody conflicts.

For an example to make a point, it needs an explanation. Theories that purport to explain why religions generate violence abound. Mark Juergensmeyer's book *Terror in the Mind of God* suggests one such explanation. A central reason why violence has accompanied religion's renewed political presence, he argues, has to do with "the nature of religious imagination, which always has had the propensity to absolutize and to project images of cosmic war." Of course, cosmic war is waged for the sake of peace, so that precisely as a phenomenon at whose core lies cosmic war "religion has been order restoring and life affirming." The problem is that religion seeks to restore order and affirm life through the violence of cosmic war. Though its intentions are good, its means are not. If religion is not to do more harm than good, it cannot be left to its own devices, argues Juergensmeyer. He does not go as far as did some Enlightenment critics, who demanded that religion be neutralized or even eliminated as a factor in public life. But he insists that religion "needs the temper of rationality and fair play that Enlightenment values give to civil society." Religion *qua* religion is inherently violent; the Enlightenment must redeem it.

Juergensmeyer is mistaken — not in affirming the values of rationality and fair play but in thinking that these values need to be introduced into religion from the outside and in implicitly suggesting that religion is bereft of additional resources to counter any tendency toward violence it may have. Take Christianity as an example — the religion I know the best and the religion whose legacy is sometimes claimed to be the most violent of all religions. Does it need to learn rationality from the Enlightenment? What about its many eminently rational figures, such as some major theologians? Is Descartes more rational than Augustine? Kant more rational than Aquinas? One must operate with a rather provincial notion of rationality to make such a claim. Does Christianity need to learn fair play from the Enlightenment? What about its members who were not only fair but truly loving, such as some of its most prominent saints? Is St. Francis less fair than Locke? Mother Teresa, with all her shortcomings, less fair than Marx? These and other theologians and saints are not anomalies in the Christian tradition at odds with the inner logic of the faith itself. They are embodiments of what is best in it.

At least when it comes to Christianity, *the cure against religiously in-*

duced or legitimized violence is not less religion, but, in a carefully qualified sense, more religion. What I mean is this: Strip religious commitments of all cognitive and moral content and reduce faith to a cultural resource endowed with a diffuse aura of the sacred, and you are likely to get religiously inspired or legitimized violence. Nurture people in the tradition and educate them about it, and if you get militants, they will be militants for peace.

Karl Barth offers good guidance on what to do in the face of the undeniable misuse of the Christian faith to foster violence. First, we need an *unflinching critique* of Christianity. It deserves critique and it can withstand critique. Attempts at damage control by theological spin doctors and ecclesiastical document shredders are not only counterproductive but also deeply offensive to the spirit of the very faith being defended. Second, we need *authentic and imaginative retrieval* of the faith. Barth's critique of Christianity as religion was in the service of rediscovering Christianity as a living faith. Ultimately, it will take such living and embodied Christian faith to show that love and not terror is on the mind of its God.

A Politician for All Seasons

During the United States elections in 2000, when it became clear that we did not yet have a president-elect, I determined not to waste time glued to the television set trying to follow the meandering route that would eventually give us our new president. Better to use the time, I thought, to reflect on the nature of democracy and the character of holders of public office. On this latter issue, a single act by Pope John Paul II has charted the course of my thinking over the past few weeks. On October 31 the pope proclaimed Sir Thomas More the patron saint of politicians. As Cardinal Roger Etchegaray explained, the pope wanted to remind politicians "of the absolute priority of God in the heart of public affairs."

The choice was — perhaps surprisingly — uncontroversial. Among church folk, Anglicans presumably had the strongest grounds for objection to the pope's decision; after all, More was profoundly opposed to their very *raison d'etre*. Yet they honor him "as somebody who took a stand for what he believed in," explained the chaplain of the Anglican All Saints Church in Rome. Even politicians did not protest the choice of their new patron saint. Were they all persuaded that they should follow More's example and obey the voice of conscience, no matter what?

A good politician, we are told, will know how to turn any situation to his or her own advantage. No wonder, then, that some of them found in More a resource for proceeding with business as usual. As Alessandra Stanley reported in the *New York Times,* some Italian politicians were quick to see in More "a model for Latin lovers." Did he not contemplate a *menage a trois* in *Utopia*? mused former Italian president Francesco

Cossiga. David Alton, a member of the English House of Lords, insisted that More would have been on his (Alton's) more liberal side on such issues as human cloning and abortion. And though he "couldn't offhand think of any colleagues willing to die for their beliefs," he rather ungallantly offered up Anne Widdicombe, a Catholic member of Parliament and a right-to-life crusader, as a potential candidate.

Governor Bush could have enlisted More after the incident of the expletive hurled at a reporter. Had not the saint-to-be used scatological language against Luther — another hero of mine, all his warts notwithstanding — and called him "shit-devil (*cocodemon*)" who was "filled with shit (*merda*), dung (*strecus*), and excrement (*coenum*)"? Luther himself, of course, was hardly at a loss for similar terminology.

I am sure John Paul II had something else than scatological language in mind when he elevated Sir Thomas More as a permanent example to public officials. More was a politician in the best sense of the word — an extraordinary man who used his immense talents for the public good. And he did what, in the culture of contemporary postindustrial societies, seems almost unimaginable: he chose to die rather than to compromise his conscience. He was a martyr.

Today we don't know what to do with martyrs. For one thing, our beliefs increasingly take the form of "changing opinions" and "shifting perspectives" rather than "firm convictions" and "enduring truth claims." Moreover, we no longer place much stock in an "afterlife" in which the rightness of our earthly actions would be validated before the ultimate judge, and so we don't see what good could come from dying for one's beliefs. More thought otherwise, and it is the power of these convictions, not just his great intellectual gifts and social skills, that made him both a great man and a great politician.

And yet when I when I read Peter Ackroyd's *Life of Thomas More*, it was not More's willingness to die for his beliefs that impressed me the most. It was rather what I would describe as his "generosity" — the kind of generosity this great man learned by meditating on the passion of Christ. Consider his last words to the court that had just sentenced him to death. The charge was that he was "attempting to deprive the king of his lawful title as supreme head of the Church of England, which is treason." As More saw it, he was not guilty since he had done nothing and said nothing regarding the issue; he had simply kept silent. After he was judged guilty, and when asked whether he had "anythinge els to alleage for your defense," he uttered these astonishing words:

> More haue I not to say, my Lordes, but that like as the blessed Apostle St. Pawle, as we read in the actes of the Apostles, was present, and consented to the death of St Stephen, and kepte their clothes that stoned him to deathe, and year be they nowe both twayne holy Sainctes in heaven, and shall continue there friends for euer, So I verily truste, and shall therefore hartelye pray, that thoughe your Lordshippes have nowe here in the earthe bine Judges to my condemnaction, we may yeat herafter in heaven meerily all meete together, to our euerlasting saluacion. . . .

More was a condemned man. He had nothing to gain by sounding a conciliatory note. And yet he not only prayed for his executioners' everlasting salvation, but also expressed his desire to meet them and be friends with them in heaven. It takes courage to die for one's beliefs — more courage than most of us have. But it takes true sainthood to desire to be "friends forever" with one's enemies. More believed that there was something larger than his outstanding political career — the good of the people, the truth of his convictions, and the love for neighbor that bridges the deepest enmity, all three values rooted in "the absolute priority of God." What a human being! What a politician!

GIVING AND FORGIVING

When Hungers Clash

His name I have forgotten, but the image of him eating at our table is indelible. Every month on the first Sunday he would make his way from the back country to the city of Novi Sad, where my father was a minister. A fellow Pentecostal, surrounded by a sea of hostile nonbelievers and Orthodox Christians, he came to our church for communion. After feasting at the Lord's Table, he joined our family for the Sunday meal.

A roughhewn figure, both intriguing and slightly menacing, he sat quietly, a bit hunched, across the table from me, then a teenage boy. A moustache that would put Nietzsche's to shame dominated his face. Even before the meal would start, my memory would play the *sound* of him eating at our table. It was the sound of my mother's soup leaping across a centimeter-wide chasm from his spoon through his moustache into his mouth. The climax of the week's menu, as Mary Douglas calls the Sunday lunch, was ruined.

"Hunger is hunger," wrote Karl Marx, "but the hunger gratified by cooked meat eaten with a knife and fork is a different hunger from that which bolts down raw meat with the aid of hand, nail and tooth." Hungers and the ways of satisfying them are thick with culture. They are laden not simply with what within a particular society lies on the spectrum between "highly cultured" and "barbaric," but also with cultural elements that separate discrete communities and protect their identities.

When our guest came, the clash of cultures played itself out as a clash of hungers. My parents never said anything, though I could sense their reservations about his manners. Yet it was also clear that they not only thought it important to invite him repeatedly, but also admired the robustness of his Christian commitment in spite of great adversity.

My parents kept extending the invitation because they thought one should not separate the Table of the Lord at which my father presided in the morning from the table of our home at whose head he was sitting at noon. I am not sure how much they knew about the original unity of the eucharistic celebration and the agape meal, but they clearly practiced their inseparability. As the Lord gave his body and blood for sinners, so we ought to be ready to share something of our very selves with strangers. The circle of our table fellowship was opened up by the wounds of Christ, and a stranger was let in.

A meal offered is a gift given. In Luke 14:12-14 Jesus says, "When you give a luncheon or a dinner, do not invite your friends or your brothers or your relatives or rich neighbors, in case they may invite you in return, and you would be repaid. But when you give a banquet, invite the poor, the crippled, the lame, and the blind. And you will be blessed, because they cannot repay you, for you will be repaid at the resurrection of the righteous." Hospitality ought not be part of an economy of exchange with superiors or equals, but of an economy of donation to the destitute and weak.

It is trite but true to say that giving is hard; we reluctantly part with our goods. But giving well is doubly hard. Every act of giving establishes a relation of asymmetry between the giver and the receiver; giving is grace, and the one who receives is dependent on and obliged to the one who gives. Marx attacked grace in the name of the recipient's independence. Nietzsche called it into question in the name of the recipient's self-respect. If these critics of grace have anything to teach, it is that the art of giving consists in knowing how to give without enslaving or humiliating the receiver.

When the gift is a shared meal, the art of giving is on the one hand made easier. The commonality of having the same elemental need satisfied with the same food around the same table diminishes the asymmetry between the giver and the receiver. At the same time, the very proximity of the receiver to the giver, who shares not only possessions but something of his or her very self, makes the giving more difficult. Since food and the customs surrounding eating are so heavily laden with culture, the proximity highlights differences between the giver and the receiver. If stark, the differences become uncomfortable, even hardly bearable. When hungers of mutual strangers clash at the same table, it is easy for condescension, even disgust, to creep into the attitude of the giver toward the receiver.

Only love will cure the giver from the tendency to despise the receiver. The critical test of love is joy in the presence of the other. With our Sunday lunch guest, we did what Jesus commanded — invite for a meal those who are unable to give in return. But did we give our gift as we should have? For myself, I was all too happy about his inability to return the favor. It was enough that we had done our duty and given him a meal; to receive a meal from him would have required virtue beyond my capacity. I was not a good enough host.

At its best, an invitation to a stranger to come to the table is a form of giving for the sake of the other — giving which, as such, does not expect a return, though it rejoices when it is "unexpectedly" given. Good givers are willing to enter the asymmetric relationship with the receiver through their giving without calculation that the giving will pay off. If they are rich or powerful, they also feel a tinge of shame about giving — shame less about what they are doing than about the way the social relations are structured, shame that the relationship is not reciprocal. And they are good givers precisely because they delight in the presence and desire the well-being of the receiver.

Difficult, Very Difficult

The most extraordinary thing associated with the surrender of the two top officials of the Khmer Rouge regime — which was responsible for the deaths of about one million people — never made it to the headlines. Reporters highlighted the perpetrators' demand to "let bygones be bygones" and the prime minister's offer to receive them with open arms. But the demand and the offer were, in a sense, no news at all. That the killers would want the dead forgotten was as predictable as it was reprehensible. Like most perpetrators, Noun Chea and Khieu Samphan wanted the best of all impunities — the erasure of memory before the misdeeds were named and condemned.

Neither was it surprising that the prime minister of Cambodia, himself a former Khmer Rouge leader, would want to welcome the killers "not with prisons and handcuffs," but with luxury suites and "bouquets of flowers." Like most authoritarian rulers, Hun Sen would rather not have things stirred up, partly to keep the population pacified, partly to avoid the searchlight of justice falling on himself.

What was truly extraordinary about the surrender and its aftermath was the reaction of some victims. "When I see them, it is difficult to forgive — very difficult," said one person who had lost most of his family during the Khmer Rouge years. "It is just like waking me up when I see them. But we have to forgive and move on." That willingness to forgive remained generally buried in the main body of reports.

Have to forgive? Many victims want to forgive even when the immensity of their suffering cries out not so much for justice as for a terrible revenge. (This seems less true of the increasingly vengeful and litigious United States than the rest of the world!) For some, the wells from which the tears flow have simply dried up, and the fuel which feeds the fires of anger has burned up; after years of mourning and rage, they are tired and want rest. Others realize that they themselves cannot be healed until they have given up resentment and moved on — with or without justice done.

Still others believe that their moral dignity will not be restored until they have come to love their enemies; they want to forgive, even to let the misdeeds fall into oblivion, because they refuse to let those who have maimed their bodies mar their souls. If they are Christians, victims will ultimately want to forgive because, as Desmond Tutu puts it, it is "a gospel imperative" that "the victims of injustice and oppression must ever be ready to forgive"; Christ demands and the Spirit empowers them to forgive as they have been forgiven.

Whatever the reasons, when forgiveness happens it is always a miracle of grace. The obstacles in its way are immense. The most difficult one is not the transgression itself, but a consistent refusal of the transgressor genuinely to repent. As a rule, transgressors will not make apologies until pressed hard, often only with their backs against the wall; Samphan's barely audible "sorry, very sorry" came only after aggressive questioning. When perpetrators reluctantly mutter their "sorry," they often show regret for what others have suffered, not remorse for what they have done; Chea seemed sorry for the lives lost in Cambodia's civil war, not for the ravages of the Khmer Rouge rule.

And when perpetrators do accept some responsibility, they quickly try to shrug it off by pointing to the comparable if not greater misdeeds of others; on the question of guilt, Samphan argued that it is difficult "to say who is wrong and who is right and who is doing this and who is doing that. . . ." Finally, all along, perpetrators will insist that it is best for all concerned not to revisit the past; after consenting that some feelings of "resentment" are normal, Samphan noted, "we have much more problems to resolve at the present and in the future and we have to forget the past."

Strange as it may sound, genuine repentance seems more difficult than forgiveness. This should not surprise those who have pondered the gravity and power of human sin. Its most notable feature is that it unfailingly refuses to *be* sin. We not only refuse to admit the wrongdoing and to accept guilt but seem neither to detest nor feel sorry about the sin committed. Given the sin's misrecognition of its own ugliness, early Reformed theology insisted that a genuine repentance before God is possible only through the work of the Holy Spirit. The same may well be true of repentance before human beings.

Perpetrators' hardness of heart notwithstanding, many victims do want to forgive (a private act distinct from, though related to, the public treatment of the perpetrators). Willingness to forgive is a testimony to the beauty of their character, for in it they are most like unto the God who in Jesus Christ died on the cross for the godless. Neither the horrendousness of the transgression nor the refusal of perpetrators to repent should take that willingness away from them.

Of course, the willingness to forgive is not yet forgiveness. Just as repentance is a mode in which we receive divine forgiveness, so repentance is a mode in which we receive human forgiveness. The unrepentant will remain unforgiven — even if it is true that God and victims forgive. Yet the gift of forgiveness should not be withdrawn from the unrepentant. Just as divine grace invites to repentance and makes repentance possible, so also victims' gift of forgiveness creates a space for perpetrators to admit their fault, ask for pardon, and mend their ways.

Will victims' gift always find fertile ground in the hearts of perpetrators? It will not. Should victims continue to extend the gift in spite of the refusal? They should — for the sake of their own dignity and health, and above all, because of the life that the one truly innocent victim, Jesus Christ, offered for the salvation of the godless world.

One-Way Giving

I f you are like me, you dread one seemingly inescapable part of Christmas celebrations: gift-giving. My problems start with shopping. To give, you have to shop, but for me shopping is disturbingly disorienting, especially at Christmas. With all the glitzy stuff staring at me from everywhere, I can't figure out what I like (let alone what I like and can also afford). But the ordeal of shopping itself is nothing compared to the challenge of finding the right kind of gift. Too expensive a gift is — well, too expensive. Too cheap a gift is insulting. The list of difficulties goes on. Christmas gift-giving becomes almost painful. And when the actual exchange of gifts takes place, it often turns into a protracted exercise in reciprocal dissimulation: phony delight, fake praise, feigned gratitude.

We all can imagine Christmas gift-giving at its best, however. The shopping is over, decent gifts are wrapped and waiting under the Christmas tree, and the long-awaited ritual begins. Each person gives and each receives. No one gives first so that others must feel obliged to return; all give and all receive at the same time (or rather each receives in his or her turn so that all can rejoice about each gift). Each person is grateful, each person is generous, and all are rejoicing. The gifts themselves are not simply things that people like, need, or desire; they are sacraments of a relationship. By giving things, givers have given their own selves.

This kind of gift-giving turns the whole ritual into a feast of delight — delight in things given, delight in acts of giving and receiving, delight in persons giving and receiving, delight in community constituted by mutual gift-giving. When we have engaged in such gift-giving, we have tasted the advent of God's new world in which love reigns. What better expression of the spirit of Christmas could there be than an enactment of a community of joyful givers and grateful receivers?

And yet there is something wrong with this account of Christmas gift-giving. I don't mean that it leaves out the most important thing about Christmas, namely that Christmas is first of all about receiving the indescribable gift of God — the God who came in human form — and only secondarily about the creation of a community of true mutual givers. Even if that is granted — as it should be — something is still wrong about celebrating Christmas only by ritually enacting a community of joyous giving and receiving. Though such a community is an earthly good almost beyond all others because it is a community of love, in a world of uneven distribution of wealth it is positively sinful for such communities to remain turned only toward themselves. The gifts may not just circle through the community to the delight of its members; they must also reach outsiders in need.

Consider two instances of gift-giving associated with Christmas in the New Testament. Take first the wise men from the East, who brought their gifts to a holy stranger to whom the star had led them. They did not huddle together around a warm fire and give gifts to each other and delight in each other's generosity. Take second the Son of God from heaven. Here is how the Apostle Paul tells the story of Christmas: "For you know the generous act of our Lord Jesus Christ, that though he was rich, yet for your sakes he became poor, so that by his poverty you might become rich" (2 Cor. 8:9).

The Son of God did not just come to reveal to humans the circle of blissful exchanges within the Holy Trinity as the model for gift-giving between humans; he divested himself of heavenly wealth and became a Holy Child so that the fragile flesh of humanity could be taken up into the embrace of the eternal God. In both of these cases, the circle of intimates opened up, and gifts left that circle to reach those in need. Gifts did not travel on a two-way street so that the closed circle of givers and receivers could delight in their exchanges; gifts traveled on a one-way street so that the needy could be helped.

Christmas celebration is about two kinds of gift-giving, not just one. It is about reciprocal giving in a circle of intimates, an enactment of a provisional advent of God's future world of love. It is also about unidirectional giving to those outside the circle of intimates, a small contribution to aligning the world of sin and need with God's coming world of love. Mostly at Christmas, we practice the first kind of giving (that is, we practice it if we succeed in resisting the temptation to make Christmas into a large festival not of mutual delight but of common greed, a season in which we use faith to justify our greed).

We might fill a shoebox with toys and other imperishable goods and send them to a destitute child across the ocean (as Samaritan's Purse, for instance, is encouraging us to do through its project Operation Christmas Child). But the lion's share of our gifts remains within the circle. Our priorities are wrong, even sinfully wrong. For Christmas is not the goal, the realization of the world of perfect love. Christmas is the movement toward that goal, the endeavor of God to draw all people into the world of love.

Here is a modest proposal for Christmas: let's give as much to those outside the circle of our intimates as we give to those who are inside it.

More Blessed to Give

S ome time ago, a family paid us a visit. Robert, as I will call a little boy who came along, was about our son's age, and neither of them had yet mastered the art of sharing. But Robert was now on Nathanael's turf. Nathanael's toys were scattered all around, and it was his responsibility to share. He did well for a while, but when he saw Robert reaching for his lawn mower, his virtuousness came to an abrupt end. He screamed and charged toward Robert to take the precious object from his hands. After intervening to end the pulling and tugging, I was just about to deliver another mini-sermon about sharing when Robert's mother beat me to it. "Nathanael," she said, "Robert was just trying to mow your lawn for you, so you don't have to do the work yourself!"

A clever and seemingly innocent remark — but I did not like it at all. Generally, I don't mind other people helping raise my child. So I did not dislike the mere fact that she said something. But I objected to *what* she said. I wanted to shout, "Don't listen to her, my son. Tell her not to manipulate you. Tell her, 'Don't package *your* son's interest as *my* good! And don't try to transmute my generosity into selfishness!'" But of course I kept quiet.

For some time now I've been troubled by the way we in contemporary societies — especially in America — motivate each other to virtuous behavior. We allow the market to shape a good deal of our everyday encounters. The market operates on the principle of exchange between self-interested parties. A company wants to sell us a product. To do so, it does not tell us, "If you get this cell phone, you'll do us a favor — we won't go out of business, many mouths will be fed and mortgage loans paid on time, and our profits will increase." Instead, a company will tell us something like this (though in different words): "This cool phone of ours is exactly what you need. It is small, user-friendly, and has all the features you want. You'll benefit from having it." We object when companies misrepresent the benefits of their products; we may also object when they seek to create new wants by persuading us with the subtlety of a good seduction that we really cannot live without what a company wants to sell us. But on the whole, we think that it is appropriate for companies to appeal to our self-interest as they pursue their own self-interest. After all, when I give out my own money I ought to get something I am interested in getting. Similarly, if I am parting with the good I have produced, I ought to get something in return.

So it is in commercial transactions, which operate on the principle of exchange. I may, of course, choose simply to give my money away. Or a company may choose to donate its products. But when this happens, we have exited the domain of economic exchange and have entered the domain of gift-giving. If I see things rightly, in contemporary societies the domain of economic exchanges is increasingly encroaching upon the domain of gift-giving. Not that gift-giving was ever easy, and some would even argue — not completely persuasively, I think — that it is impossible. That's why Jesus had to instruct his disciples not to transmute what is to be a gift into an exchange of commodities. In relation to the gift of hospitality he said:

> When you give a luncheon or a dinner, do not invite your friends or your brothers or your relatives or rich neighbors, in case they may invite you in return, and you would be repaid. But when you give a banquet, invite the poor, the crippled, the lame, and the blind. And you will be blessed, because they cannot repay you, for you will be repaid at the resurrection of the righteous. (Luke 14:12-14)

At its best, hospitality belongs not to the domain of exchange but to the domain of gift-giving. We ought not expect to get as much (or more) out of hospitality as we put in. Every time exchange threatens to subvert what ought to be a gift, we should offer resistance. That's where learning to share a toy with a guest comes in.

Notice how deeply at odds were the words of Robert's well-meaning but misguided mom with what she was trying to do — to help Nathanael learn how to share. First she construed what was clearly and exclusively in Robert's interest as a good Robert was doing to Nathanael. This was a manifest misrepresentation. A pattern of such misrepresentations would have the effect of making Nathanael wonder whether people actually do good to one another rather than pursuing their own self-interests under the guise of gift-giving.

Second, she construed the good she wanted Nathanael to do for Robert as a good Nathanael was doing for himself. In effect, she was robbing Nathanael of the opportunity to give Robert a gift and therefore truly to share. Tomorrow he might think to himself, "Why should I do for others what is clearly not in my own interest if my magnanimity will be interpreted as selfishness?"

It may be hard to teach our children and motivate ourselves to give to others without appealing to our self-interest. But something of our human and Christian excellence depends on whether we succeed or not. It is still more blessed to give than to receive.

All about Getting?

Will 9/11 have any consequences for how we celebrate Christmas? The pain of absence will be more intense for those who have lost loved ones. The struggle for survival will cloud the joy of many New York owners of small businesses and their families. But will the terrorist attack change anything about the "spirit" in which we celebrate? We are tempted to respond with a defiant "no." "Enough for the evildoers to have snuffed out the lives of our fellow citizens and destroyed our property. We won't let them tamper with the dearest of our feasts — Christmas. Life must go on as usual." But maybe life should *not* go on as usual, at least not in the way we celebrate Christmas. The fires that melted down the Twin Towers exposed powerfully the fragility of our lives. Faced with death, we maybe caught a glimpse of what otherwise tends to remain hidden from our sight: the ultimate meaninglessness of a consumerist culture.

As I was driving to work recently, a segment of a song caught my attention. In country-music style I was treated to a theological lesson: God is our Santa Claus "each and every day." The words, sung in a half self-satisfied, half whinily wistful tone, got me thinking. I had a flashback of my three-and-a-half-year-old son's big eyes as he was rattling off his Christmas wish list: "I want a forklift, and a cane so I can walk like an old man, a dog-bone, and . . . hey, Dad, you know what — I also want a saxophone and a trumpet." Long-stored images of frenzied Christmas shoppers resurfaced in my brain — human beings, like giant ants, racing in all directions and returning home with more stuff than they could carry. Christmas, it seems, is all about getting. The God whose coming into history we celebrate at Christmas must therefore be like Santa — all ears to hear every one of our wishes, and with a bottomless bag full of gifts. A Santa Claus god for a Santa Claus culture?

". . . And a sword will pierce your own soul too." This is what the old man on whom God's Spirit rested told Mary, the mother of Jesus, as he was holding her infant. The sword in Mary's soul was not just the coming conflict surrounding the mission of Jesus. It was the nails that pierced his body and held it to the cross. So Christmas is about an infant born for a mission that will, in the end, take him to a cruel death.

Many things are puzzling about the perpetrators of the 9/11 attack. What borders almost on the unintelligible is that relatively well educated and prosperous men would methodically plan over a period of months not simply to kill others for a cause but also to kill themselves in the process. Their own death was not just a possible, or even a likely, outcome of their mission. The only way to accomplish it was to be killed. The act of killing thousands of innocent people is profoundly evil, and so we rightly abhor it. But at some level we understand it; for unfortunately, people who would do almost anything to *get* their way are not rare. That somehow fits our Santa Claus culture with its Santa Claus god. So killing others we understand, even if we are deeply troubled by it. But we don't understand killing oneself. Our key values are freedom and possession, *my* freedom and *my* possession. So we're baffled by someone who *gives his life* for a cause. Most of us don't live for anything larger than ourselves and therefore cannot fathom dying for anything, except maybe to protect our freedoms and possessions.

Imagine that on December 23 you heard a man in a busy shopping mall crying out to the crowds: "Repent, repent! Close this place down! Give up your phony and self-serving exchange of gifts! It is not Christmas that you are celebrating. You self-obsessed little brats, you are just after more toys and candies." If you heard this outcry, you'd call the police because you'd think that the man was deranged. Yet like a court fool, he'd be partly right. Jesus was the Christ because he lived and died for something larger than himself — for the love of God and humanity, to give life to others, not to take it away. It is the birth of this man, this God-man, that we celebrate at Christmas — which should serve as a reminder that our lives are meaningful to the extent that we turn away from ourselves and live for God and neighbor.

HOPE AND RECONCILIATION

Black Milk of Daybreak

Fifty years ago in Bucharest, a young Jewish poet wrote a poem with unpredictable rhythms and grim metaphors, and a startling mixture of tenderness and brutality. Here is the first stanza:

> Black milk of daybreak we drink it at evening
> we drink it at midday and morning we drink it at night
> we drink and we drink
> we shovel a grave in the air there you won't lie too cramped
> A man lives in the house he plays with his vipers he writes
>   he writes when it grows dark to Deutschland your golden
>   hair Margareta
>   he writes it and steps out of doors and the stars are all sparkling
>   he
>   whistles his hounds to come close
> he whistles his Jews into rows has them shovel a grave in the
>   ground
> he commands us play up for the dance.

This poem must be one of the most remarkable literary creations about the most infamous event in the twentieth century. The event is the Holocaust; the poem is Paul Celan's "Deathfugue." Behind the outlandish lyric about digging "graves" in the air and in the ground and about "playing up for the dance" lies a brutal reality. It was a common practice in Nazi concentration camps to order one group of prisoners to play or sing nostalgic tunes while others dug graves or were executed. Young German men who were cultivated enough to occupy themselves with writing and who were tender enough to daydream about their girlfriends' golden hair were masters of death.

The Holocaust may be unique in the combination of barbarity and civilization, primitivism and sophistication in its perpetrators; it may be unique in the scale of murders committed; and it may be unique in the single-mindedness and technological skill with which genocidal intentions were directed against a single people, the Jews. But in many respects the Holocaust is not an anomaly in the world we live in. Death is not just a blue-eyed master "aus Deutschland." Rivers of blood and mountains of corpses — most recently in Bosnia and Rwanda — are a horrid testimony to the fact that the world we live in is a world in which, in many places, the practice of the most brutal exclusion is the order of the day.

There are no signs that the practice of exclusion is a short, dark tunnel at whose end lies a bright light of social harmony. Rapid population growth, diminishing resources, unemployment, migration to shanty cities, and lack of education are steadily increasing pressure among the many social fault lines of our globe. Though we cannot predict exactly when and where social quakes will occur or how powerful they will be, we can be sure that the earth will shake.

As the image of "fault lines" suggests, clashes will take place along the boundary lines of social groups. Today, after the breakdown of a bipolar world, social tectonic plates are defined less by ideology than by culture. Conditions are ripe for more Rwandas and Bosnias in the future. And when Rwandas and Bosnias happen, a cold night envelops social landscapes, a night that lures us into "the works of darkness" (Rom. 13:12) because it speaks to our sinister propensities. Many a person will find her cup filled with the black milk of daybreak.

"Deathfugue" ends with the following lines: "your golden hair Margareta / your ashen hair Shulamith." Margareta is the blond-haired German girl — the romantic ideal drawn from Goethe's poetry — of whom the SS executioner tenderly daydreams. Shulamith is no "ash blond but the 'black and comely' maiden in the Song of Songs. . . . Shulamith is the beloved par excellence and is seen as the Jewish people itself," writes Celan's biographer, John Felstiner. At the end of his comments on "Deathfugue" Felstiner notes that when Celan twins Shulamith with Margareta, "nothing can reconcile them. Celan's word *aschenes* — ashen hair of Shulamith — tells why."

If Celan leaves Margareta and Shulamith unreconciled side by side as symbols of the unbridgeable gulf between the Jews and the Germans created by unspeakable evil, who can blame him? When he wrote "Deathfugue," the ovens that sent millions of his compatriots, including his parents, to their "grave in the air" had barely cooled down. But what about the followers of Jesus Christ, the Messiah who died for us the ungodly, those who, just like St. Paul before his encounter with the risen Christ, in our own way persecute others, enter "house after house" and drag people off to prisons, ravage whole communities?

"Deathfugue" is a kind of mission statement in reverse, a poetic narration of what we do when, instead of seeking to practice a "heaven" in which the love of God and neighbor reigns, we are bent on creating a "hell" in which God is blasphemed because human beings are despised and brutalized. A testimony of atrocity and grief, "Deathfugue" is a reminder that in a world of exclusion — a world we ourselves keep recreating because it is a world so deeply entrenched in our very hearts — we need to learn to practice embrace.

The reconciliation of sinful humanity to God is at the heart of the gospel we proclaim; the reconciliation between human beings estranged on account of injustice, deception, and violence must be at the center of the mission we pursue (see Ephesians 2). We should not rest until Margareta and Shulamith, blacks and whites, "decent citizens" and "strange intruders" from abroad who muddy the purity of cultural spaces have extended their arms to each other in joyful embrace.

A Cup of Coffee

In his moving and profound account of the war in Bosnia, the much-acclaimed Bosnian journalist Zlatko Dizdarevic relates a story about a three-year-old girl in Sarajevo who was hit by a sniper's bullet while playing outside her home.

> Her horrified father carries her to the hospital. Bleeding, she hovers between life and death. Only after her father, a big hulk of a man, has found a doctor to care for her does he allow himself to burst into tears. The television camera records his words. These words, every one of them, belong in an anthology of humanism, helplessness, and forgiveness at its most extreme — not so much forgiving the criminal who shot a three-year-old child, as forgiving the wild beasts for being wild beasts, for being debased by an evil that destroys every human impulse. Two of his sentences accompany thoughts that will linger long past today or tomorrow. The first comes when the stricken father invites the unknown assassin to have a cup of coffee with him so that he can tell him, like a human being, what has brought him to do such a thing. Then he says, aware that this question may not elicit any human response: "One day her tears will catch up with him."

After relating this story, Dizdarevic offers the following comment, surprising in its negative assessment of the father's offer.

> There is absolutely nothing to be done for this nation. It will never attain justice and happiness if it cannot bring itself to recognize an exe-

cutioner as an executioner, a murderer as a murderer, a criminal as a criminal. If the most barbaric act imaginable in this war, a sniper shooting at a three-year-old girl playing in front of her own home, elicits only an invitation to a cup of coffee and hope for forgiveness, then Bosnia-Herzegovina doesn't stand much chance to survive.

The murderous act of deliberately shooting a three-year-old demands strict and unmerciful punishment, not an offer of understanding and forgiveness, reasons Dizdarevic. Wild beasts — those whose every human impulse has been destroyed by evil — must be tracked down and then either killed or driven out, not invited to participate in a ritual of friendship. Without punishment of the evildoers and banishment of the wild beasts, Bosnia will attain neither justice nor happiness.

I want to propose a different reading of this story. No, I am not about to suggest that the executioner should not be recognized and named as an executioner. Murder cannot be simply disregarded; the truth must be told and justice established. No, I am not about to argue that the perpetrators should be allowed to continue with their atrocities until they are persuaded by the power of forgiveness. The instruments of evil must be taken out of their hands. But I do believe that the best way — the Christian way — to respond to iron and blood is not with iron and blood.

The hope for the Bosnias of our whole world, infested as it is by exclusion, lies precisely in men and women who, despite the outrage committed against them, will muster enough strength to want to invite the perpetrator for a cup of coffee and inquire of him, as a human being, what has "brought him to do such a thing." The hope for the Bosnias of our world lies in those who believe in the power of tears to catch up with the enemy, because they are persuaded, as E. M. Cioran puts it, that tears are not "swallowed up by the earth" but "by paths unknown to us, they all go upwards." The hope for the Bosnias of our world lies in those who, despite the humiliation and suffering they have endured, have not given up on the will to embrace the enemy.

Why should one embark upon the difficult road toward embrace in the midst of raging exclusion? Because we must resist being sucked into the vortex of inhumanity. "The rifle butt in the back," correctly writes Dizdarevic elsewhere in the book, "shatters everything civilization has ever accomplished, removes all finer human sentiments, and wipes out any sense of justice, compassion, and forgiveness." If the rifle butt in the back of the victim creates inhumanity, then hope cannot lie in a rifle butt in the back of the perpetrator; for this would only ensure the triumph of inhumanity — a sense "of justice, compassion, and forgiveness" will have given way to the rage of revenge and hatred. The hope for the Bosnias of our world lies instead with men and women who are determined to fight evil every step of the way while refusing to let the rifle butt do its work on their *souls* once it is finished doing its work on their bodies.

The refusal of victims to let violence committed against them contaminate their souls must be one of the most difficult and most heroic acts of which a human being is capable. Dizdarevic slights it by describing the response of the father as "*only* an invitation to a cup of coffee and hope for forgiveness" (italics added). Does he think that the father does not condemn the act? Does he think that the father had no rage to attend to before the invitation was offered? Does he not see what a superhuman effort it would take to look the assassin in the eye and ask "Why?" instead of letting the flood of legitimate accusations flow?

Without heroism that seeks to offer forgiveness while not dispensing it glibly, and heroism that strives to establish communion while not condoning evil — without such heroism, which reflects the very heart of the Triune God, we may be doomed, in Paul Celan's words, to "drink the black milk of daybreak, to drink it at evening, to drink it at midday and morning, to drink it at night, to drink it and drink it."

The Core of the Faith

At the very beginning of her book *Reconciled Being: Love in Chaos,* President Mary McAleese of Ireland highlights the words of the Apostle Paul: "All this has been the work of God. He has reconciled us unto himself through Christ and has enlisted us in this ministry of reconciliation" (2 Cor. 5:18). For her, reconciliation is not simply an event between "the soul and its God"; it has social and political dimensions.

For centuries, Christians have been hesitant to make this move. Hence the Christian tradition offers very little wisdom on the social meaning of reconciliation. The omission is pernicious. Partly because they privatized reconciliation, churches were often impotent with respect to their people's conflicts and became accomplices in heinous crimes. The omission is also baffling. For Paul, reconciliation between people is not an add-on to the reconciliation of humanity to God, but part and parcel of it.

The best way to explicate this intricate connection between reconciliation with God and among human beings is to peek into the origins of Paul's theology of reconciliation. Seyoon Kim argues that Paul's notion of reconciliation "grew out of his own theological reflections on his Damascus road conversion experience. This thesis explains, more plausibly than any other," he goes on to say,

> the fundamental innovation that Paul made in the Jewish idea of reconciliation — that is, that it is not human beings who reconcile an angry God to themselves . . . rather, it is God who reconciles human beings to himself through the atoning death of Jesus Christ. For on the

189

Damascus road Paul, who came to see himself as God's enemy in his activities before Damascus, experienced God's reconciling action, which brought forgiveness of sins and the making of a new creation by his grace.

If Kim is right, four significant features of reconciliation emerge with clarity. First, as a persecutor of the church Paul was an enemy of God. In conversion Paul encountered God, who was not wrathful, as God might have been, but instead showed love by offering to reconcile Paul, the enemy. Paul's conversion was not the result of pursuing strict justice on the part of the "victim." Had the "victim" pursued justice, Paul would never have become the apostle of the very church he was persecuting. Paul was saved through the gift of divine grace by which God sought to reconcile the enemy.

No cheap reconciliation that shuts its eyes to injustice took place on the road to Damascus, however. The divine voice called the action by its proper name — "persecution" — and asked the uncomfortable "Why?" "Saul, Saul, why do you persecute me?" (Acts 9:4). Jesus Christ, the victim, named the injustice and made the accusation in the very act of offering forgiveness.

Second, if the origin of Paul's message of reconciliation was his encounter with the risen Christ on the road to Damascus, then the enmity toward God — the human trespasses God does not hold against us on account of the atoning death of Christ — does not consist in isolated attitudes and acts toward God, which then, as a consequence, result in enmity toward other human beings. Paul was "breathing threats and murder against the disciples of the Lord" (Acts 9:1). At the same time, the voice from heaven identified itself as the voice of Jesus Christ: "I am Jesus, whom you are persecuting" (Acts 9:4-5). So from the start and at its heart, enmity toward God is enmity toward a concrete community, and enmity toward a concrete community is enmity toward God. As a consequence, reconciliation has not only a vertical but also a horizontal dimension. It contains a turn away from enmity toward people, not just from enmity to God, and it contains embrace of a community — precisely that community which was the target of enmity.

Third, inscribed in the narrative of the very event that transformed

Paul from persecutor to apostle was the message that he came to proclaim — that God "justifies the ungodly" (Rom. 4:5), that we were reconciled to God "while we were enemies" (Rom. 5:10). At the core of the doctrine of reconciliation lies the belief that the offer of reconciliation is not based on justice done and the cause of enmity removed. Rather, the offer of reconciliation is a way of justifying the unjust and *overcoming* the opponents' enmity — not so as to condone their injustice and affirm their enmity, but to open up the possibility of *doing* justice and living in peace, whose ultimate shape is a community of love.

Fourth, the apostle of divine reconciliation became the apostle of human reconciliation too. Just as grace lies at the core of his message of divine reconciliation, so grace — whose essential dimension is affirmation of the transcended justice — lies at the core of his mission to reconcile Jews and Gentiles. Moreover, Paul argued that the pattern of divine reconciliatory movement toward estranged humanity is the model of how Christians should relate to their enemies (see Rom. 15:7). It is no accident that in the circle around Paul a grand vision of reconciliation was conceived: "For in him [Christ] all the fullness of God was pleased to dwell, and through him God was pleased to reconcile to himself all things, whether on earth or in heaven, by making peace through the blood of his cross" (Col. 1:19-20).

A vision of reconciliation — a vision that entails a coherent set of beliefs about the nature of God and of human beings and about the relation between justice and love — lies at the core of the Christian faith. If social engagement is to be properly Christian, it must be governed by this vision. And only if social engagement is governed by this vision will churches have adequate theological resources to resist the temptation to become accomplices in conflicts and instead to function as agents of peace.

Piercing the Heart

H e was sitting quietly, almost impassively, as I talked to a group of people gathered in Zagreb at the launching of the Croatian translation of my book *Exclusion and Embrace*. The forcefulness and impatience with which he later asked his question as he brought the book to be signed took me by surprise. "But where does that will come from, that will to embrace the enemy?"

I had just finished explaining one of the central claims of the book. I had argued that truth, justice, and peace between human beings are unavailable without the will to embrace the other. Moreover, the will to embrace must precede any "truth" about others and any construction of their "justice." In a sense, everything in my argument depended on that will, but I said nothing about how to acquire or sustain it; I simply assumed it.

"Is it instinctive?" he inquired.

"No, instinctive would not be quite the right word, but you are getting at something important with that term . . . ," I said somewhat haltingly. He interrupted me.

"So what then? Can one learn to want to embrace the evildoer?"

"Yes, one can learn to will rightly. . . ." As I was responding, my mind was following another train of thought. "To learn," I reasoned, "a student has to be willing to learn. But what if the student is unwilling?" I was back at the original problem. Moving full circle back to my interlocutor's initial question, I heard myself talking to him about engaging in spiritual disciplines such as prayer and the reading of the scriptures, about seeking communities that practice embrace, and about studying the lives of the saints. But the look in his eyes told me what I knew well myself. What I said might be important, but I had not answered his question; I had only removed the problem one step further. A person has to *want* to engage in spiritual disciplines, has to *want* to seek out communities that practice embrace.

Other people were pressing to the front, so my conversation with him ended. But the problem of the will that wills not what it ought remained with me.

Reflecting on his own inner struggle, the Apostle Paul wrote: "For I do not do what I want but I do the very thing I hate." From the perspective of my questioner, Paul had it easy: he was captive to sin he did not want to commit. My interlocutor's question was implying something more radical: a willing captivity to sin. At issue was not simply the inability to do the good, but the unwillingness even to attempt doing it. It is difficult enough when people are internally divided and do what they would rather not. But sometimes they seem at one with themselves in not doing good or even in doing evil.

The next morning a journalist asked basically the same question. "How can we acquire the desire for reconciliation? How can we sincerely and simply desire to embrace the enemy?" I talked to her about the human propensity to let that desire be buried under the mass of negative images and experiences generated in conflicts. We let the inner logic of the struggle dominate our actions and attitudes, a logic that demands that we see enemies only as enemies so that we can fight and finally overcome them. I implied that we all possess the will to embrace the other as an aspect of the desire for good implanted in us by our Creator. But conflicts with others generate and intensify a struggle within ourselves in which the will to exclusion often wins and crowds out the will to embrace.

In his *Confessions,* St. Augustine reflects autobiographically about such a perversion of the will. He recalls being "tied down not by irons outside myself, but my own iron will. The Enemy had control of the power of my will and from it he had fashioned a chain for me and had bound me in it." By capturing the will, the Enemy had enslaved the very principle of the self's freedom. The will willed wrongly, and so became captive to the evil it willed. What can free the captive will? When the will is bent on exclusion, what can turn it toward embrace? This was the question of my impatient interlocutor, a question I did not get to address.

Ultimately, the only answer possible is the one Augustine gave. Addressing God, he wrote about his conversion, "Thou hadst pierced our heart with the arrow of Thy charity." Liberation of the will by a piercing of the heart? Love as the instrument of piercing? Piercing must take place if the walls of the dungeon in which the will has incarcerated itself are to be broken and the will freed. But if the heart is not to be violated, love will have to do the piercing — ultimately, divine love, which comes not only from the outside but is always also inside the dungeon, tearing at its walls and striving to transmute the will to exclude into the will to embrace.

Elsewhere Augustine describes the liberation of his will as follows: "Yet Thou, O Lord, art good and merciful and didst not look propitiously upon the depths of my death and didst empty out with Thy right hand the sea of corruption from the lowest region of my heart. And this Thy whole gift was, to nill what I willed, and to will what Thou willedst."

The next time I am asked about the origin of the will to embrace, I'll repeat everything I said to my two dialogue partners from Zagreb. But in the same breath I'll also talk about the freeing of our wills by the love which God has shown to us in that Christ died for us "while we were still sinners" and which was "poured into our hearts through the Holy Spirit."

Kneeling to Remember

It was Memorial Day, and I was sitting in the church of General George S. Patton. Well, it was not quite his church, but his family had erected a monument to him in the churchyard and smuggled in a stained-glass window depicting an object or two dear to the general's heart and indispensable for the general's trade.

A few sentences into the sermon it became clear that the rector was unintimidated by the "military presence" on the church's premises. In a world drenched in violence, he insisted, the church of Jesus Christ has not condemned violence with sufficient clarity and force. The sermon was heading the right direction, I thought. Being a certain kind of near-pacifist, I felt comfortable, the general's stained-glass window right above my head notwithstanding. But my mind was unruly and wandered elsewhere — though my bad conscience kept returning it to its proper place. A fine Memorial Day sermon served as an occasion to explore connections between memory and violence.

The first station of my explorations was Elie Wiesel's memoirs, *All Rivers Run to the Sea,* which I had read a year or so before. Stating the reason for the book, he writes: "I am 66 years old, and I belong to a generation obsessed by a thirst to retain and transmit everything. For no other has the commandment Zachor — 'Remember!' — had such meaning." Why this obsession with memory? Because the memory of death will serve as a shield against death, argues Wiesel. Salvation, he wrote elsewhere, "can be found only in memory." A bit overstated, I thought, but basically right, provided one understands it rightly.

I was startled, however, to come across the following lines on the next page: "Certain events will be omitted [from the memoirs], especially those episodes that might embarrass friends, and, of course, those that might damage the Jewish people." The "everything" Wiesel is obsessed to retain and transmit explicitly excludes what "might damage the Jewish people." So salvation lies not in memory, but in remembering certain things for the good of certain people and in suppressing other things that might harm them. On the whole, this seems understandable.

But what if some memories are perceived as beneficial by one group and as damaging by another? Inversely, what if suppressing certain things is seen as healing by some people but as wounding by others? Would not then politics be the master of memory? Even more disturbing, would not such a notion of the value of memory blur the boundary between memory as a shield against death and memory as a weapon of destruction?

Wiesel's tying of memory to the good of a particular people led me to the next station on my explorations. By now the rector was well into explaining that a clear and forceful condemnation of violence by the church does not necessarily entail giving up all use of violence. I understood him to suggest a position roughly similar to Bonhoeffer's under the Nazi regime: there are situations — rare situations! — in which you must engage in violent struggle, but when you do so you must repent for having done wrong in the very act of doing what is right.

I said an "Amen" to myself, and my irreverent mind went to the recent Vatican document about the Holocaust, "We Remember: A Reflection on the Shoah." The Roman Catholic Church has, through its official organs, engaged in remembering the same events the Jewish people also seek to remember. The document makes a helpful distinction between the general anti-Jewish attitudes and practices over the centuries in "Christian" Europe and the specific form of anti-Semitism practiced with such brutality by the Nazis. But I was disturbed by its unwillingness to admit to a significant connection between the two. The Shoah, the document states, "was the work of a thoroughly modern neopagan regime. Its anti-Semitism had its roots outside of Christianity."

This is right in what it says but wrong in what it implies, or so it seems to me. The disjunction between anti-Judaism and anti-Semitism strikes me as implausible and unfortunate. I could not help wondering whether in this document the Catholic Church is unwilling to remember what "might damage the church." If so, for many Jews that very unwillingness seems damaging to the Jewish people.

By now the rector was talking about remembering those who died in American wars. And again, spurred by the sermon, my mind wandered. Wiesel is right: we must remember, at least for the time being. But how should we remember so that our memory will heal not only us but also our relationships with our neighbors? If we must unambiguously condemn violence and yet are sometimes obliged to engage in it, what is the right way to remember violence suffered and violence inflicted?

We must keep in mind that even in the most "just" deployments of violence the triumph of justice is always paid for by the practice of injustice, that bravery goes hand in hand with culpable cruelty, and that great victories involve many small and large moral defeats. And, of course, we must also remember acts of violence committed in shameful and morally abhorrent ways. The only way to remember rightly is not to shy away from remembering what is damaging to us and our own people. If we want memory to heal us and our relationships, we will have to let it wound us, let it speak to us unhindered of the wrongs we have committed.

As we were preparing to celebrate the Eucharist, it occurred to me that the best place to remember violence inflicted and suffered may be at the altar, kneeling in readiness to receive the body that was broken and the blood that was shed — for our transgressions.*

---

* For an exploration of these themes, see Miroslav Volf, *The End of Memory: Remembering Rightly in a Violent World* (Grand Rapids: Eerdmans, 2006).

A Letter to Timothy McVeigh

Dear Timothy,

As I was preparing a brief meditation on the "last words" of Jesus, I thought of you. The rector of my church asked me to speak about the "second word": "Truly I tell you, today you will be with me in paradise." If you know your Bible you will remember that Jesus said this to one of the criminals who was crucified with him. You will be executed on May 16. So I wondered what Jesus would have said to you.

Astonishing, isn't it, this "word" of Jesus? After all, the one to whom he said this had apparently committed a crime that deserved the most severe punishment available then, crucifixion. At least that is what the poor man thought: "We are getting what our deeds deserve," he rebuked his fellow criminal as the latter mocked Jesus. What is astonishing is that Jesus did not respond, "Well, I know that hanging on the cross is not pleasant, but that's how it should be: evil deeds should catch up with their doer." Instead, Jesus promised the man paradise, not in a distant future but "today," and this for nothing more than a request that Jesus remember him when he, Jesus, came into his kingdom. That the innocent end up in paradise: that's what we would expect. But that proven criminals go there too? That's surprising — at least for those who judge only by appearances and deeds.

Some people are deeply troubled by the idea that Jesus would fling the gates of paradise so wide open. What kind of paradise could it be in which criminals live and flourish together with their victims? The newspapers on this past Good Friday — the day I was to speak at my church — reported that the United States attorney general granted permission to the relatives of your victims to watch your execution. They will not have a sense of closure, some said, until they see you, the killer of their loved ones, dead. For them, closure requires that the scales of justice be balanced, and that in turn demands a punishment commensurate with the crime. I understand their feelings; many people who have been violated feel the same way.

Yet Jesus spoke of a different "closure." On the cross, Jesus provided an alternative to retribution. It is called grace. By grace, self-confessed criminals, not just good people, belong in paradise.

I know the victims will object: "Then hasn't Jesus simply thrown justice out the window?" The answer is no. After all, the criminal himself stated that he deserved punishment. He affirmed the claims of justice, even if he had transgressed against them. It is important that you do the same. According to the papers, you are not remorseful. I take this to mean that you don't think what you did was wrong.

I hope that you will not remain defiant in your last hour. You will be permitted to make a brief final statement before the lethal chemicals are administered. The relatives of the victims will be watching you. Tell them that what you did was wrong, that you are sorry for the pain you caused them. Above all, tell God that you have wronged God by violating the crown of creation. Recognition of our wrongdoing is partly how we receive from God more, much more, than we deserve — entrance into a world of love. And who knows? By such recognition, you may help "redeem" those who find it hard to live without seeing you die. For buried beneath the rubble of our sinful lust for vengeance is the desire for the closure of reconciliation, not the closure of retribution; the closure of transformed life, not the closure of death.

The executioners of the federal government will do their job — you will be put to death whether or not you admit your guilt, seek forgiveness from God and your victims, and manifest a changed life. I think the government is making a big mistake. I don't mean that the government's punishment is in principle incompatible with Christ's forgiveness. I mean that capital punishment is wrong — not as wrong as the killing of innocent people, but a serious wrong nonetheless. Yet we can't do much about that at this point, certainly not before May 16. Soon you will face the dark hour of your death. If you believe and listen intently, there you will hear Jesus tell you, "Today you will be with me in paradise."

But Jesus offers you more than a paradisiacal future. The other side of the promise "You will be with me in paradise" is his assurance "I am now with you in your hell." If you have any churchgoing in your background, you may remember that the Bible and the Apostles' Creed speak of Jesus' "descending into hell." Martin Luther, the Protestant Reformer, thought that Jesus' descent into hell did not happen after Jesus died, but as he was hanging on the cross. The cross was his hell: the hell of excruciating pain, the hell of deep disappointment, the hell of abandonment by God and friends, the hell of dark despair, the hell of taking upon himself the sin of the world — my sin and yours. The Son of God entered our hell, and he promises to lead us into paradise. Again if you believe and listen, this is what you will hear Jesus tell you in your last hour: "You are about to walk through the valley of the shadow of death. I have already been where you are now about to go. I know your dread and I want to carry away the burden of your guilt. . . . Today you will be with me in paradise."

Timothy, we have never met, and we are not likely to meet in this life. But I will look for you in paradise.

Redeeming the Past?

Lawrence Langer explains in *Holocaust Testimonies: The Ruins of Memory* that written accounts of life in the Nazi concentration camps often seek to integrate the Holocaust experience into a larger structure of meaning. The Holocaust then becomes a testimony to the "indomitable human spirit," an example of growing through suffering, a proof that moral integrity is possible even under extreme duress, a source of a more informed sense of ourselves as human beings, and so on. Oral testimonies, on the other hand, show that in the lived memory of the survivors, the Holocaust experience refuses to be tamed and appears, instead, to be something that cannot be integrated into a larger narrative of meaningful life.

Consider the dilemma of Abraham P. When he and his family arrived at Auschwitz from Hungary, his parents were sent to the left (to their death) while he, two older brothers, and a younger brother were sent to the right. Abraham P. recalls:

> I told my little kid brother, I said to him, "Solly, go to poppa and momma." And like a little kid, he followed — he did. Little did I know that I sent him to the crematorium. I am . . . I feel like I killed him. . . . I wonder what my mother and father were thinking, especially when they were all . . . , when they all went into the crematorium. I can't get it out of my head. It hurts me, it bothers me and I don't know what to do.

Can one give meaning to this experience? Not according to Langer. "Harmony and integration," he argues, "are not only impossible — they are not desirable."

But can we afford to reject integration and harmony? With Langer, I believe that we must. And yet it is difficult for us to do so, partly because, over the course of past decades, we have come to believe that our identity has a narrative structure. Consider Charles Taylor's *Sources of the Self: The Making of Modern Identity*. He claims that, as a basic condition of making sense of ourselves, we must "grasp our lives in a narrative":

> We want our lives to have meaning, or weight or substance, or to grow towards some fullness.... But this means our whole lives. If necessary, we want the future to "redeem" the past, to make it part of a life story which has sense or purpose, to take it up in a meaningful unity.

It is not only philosophers who tell us of our urge to integrate our whole past life into a meaningful unity. A good deal of trauma literature echoes the same idea. In *Traumatic Stress: The Effects of Overwhelming Experience on Mind, Body and Society*, Basel A. Van der Kolk and Alexander C. McFarlane argue that since patients cannot change their past, traumatic memories must be "placed in their proper context and reconstructed in a personally meaningful way." In other words, "giving meaning is a central goal of therapy." But should it be? Holocaust testimonies strongly urge us against this move. They tell of experiences that stubbornly refuse to be integrated into a meaningful whole.

Just the other day I was talking about these issues with a group of pastors. One of them suggested that we should not think so much of "events" and "experiences" as being redeemed, but of people as redeemed. So it is in a good deal of the Christian tradition. Think of Gregory of Nyssa and his vision of the eschatological movement of the soul — a soul which, like the Apostle Paul in Philippians 3, forgets what is behind and stretches itself out toward that infinite ocean which is God. Such a soul, says Gregory, "no longer gives any place in itself either to hope or to memory. It has what it was hoping for, and it drives out memory from its mind in its occupation with the enjoyment of good things."

Or think of Luther's "wonderful exchange" between Christ the bridegroom and Christian the bride in *The Freedom of a Christian*:

He suffered, died and descended into hell that he might overcome them all. Now since it was such a one who did all this, and death and hell could not swallow him up, these were necessarily swallowed up by him in a mighty duel; for his righteousness is greater than the sins of all men, his life stronger than death, his salvation more invincible than hell.

Narrative integration into a larger framework of meaning? Nothing of the sort! In Gregory's account of salvation, memory of the past is not given meaning but driven from the mind. In Luther's account, sin — along with death and hell — are not taken up into a meaningful unity but swallowed up by Christ. If wounded and sinful people are to find redemption, they need a robust understanding of salvation, one in which "driving out" and "overcoming" play no less important a role than "integrating" and "harmonizing."

Reconciled in the End

As the end of the second millennium approached, many Christians were preoccupied with questions that concern the end of the world. There is one important eschatological theme on which they were unlikely to have directed a single thought or heard a single word.

When asked whether it is true that one day in heaven we will see our loved ones, Karl Barth is reported to have responded, "Not only the loved ones!" The sting of the great theologian's response — be ready to meet even those whom you dislike here on earth — is more than just a personal challenge. It contains a serious and, as it turns out, inadequately addressed theological problem.

How can those who have disliked or even had good reasons to hate each other here come to inhabit together what is claimed to be, in Jonathan Edwards's memorable phrase, "a world of love"? The not-loved ones will have to be transformed into the loved ones, and those who do not love will have to begin to do so. Enemies will have to become friends.

A sense that such a social transformation is a condition of "heavenly" existence may lie behind a funeral practice in Germany in which a kind of postmortem reconciliation between the deceased and his or her enemies is enacted in the form of prayer. Participants in the burial service remember, before God, those whom the deceased may have wronged or those who may have wronged the deceased.

Popular piety is also aware of the issue. In tightly knit Christian communities one sometimes hears the injunction that their members had better learn to love each other now since they will spend eternity together. Sometime between a shadowy history and an eternity bathed in light, somewhere between this world and the coming world of perfect love, a transformation of persons and their complex relationships needs to take place. Without such transformation the world to come would not be a world of perfect love but only a repetition of a world in which, at best, the purest of loves falter and, at worst, cold indifference reigns and deadly hatreds easily flare up.

Traditionally, the last judgment along with the resurrection of the dead was taken to be the site of the transition from this world to the world to come. But if the need for the transformation of persons as well as of their complex relationships is a real one, the question is whether the last judgment, as usually conceived, can carry this weight. Consider Martin Luther. Of the various candidates from the Christian tradition, his understanding of the last judgment is most likely to constitute a kind of transition from this world to the world of perfect love.

The idea of judgment according to works, which dominated the tradition, is not absent in Luther's thought, but is integrated into the overarching judgment of grace. For believers, the last judgment is not so much a process by which the moral quality of human deeds is made unmistakably manifest and appropriate rewards and punishments apportioned, but rather, and above all, an event in which sinners are forgiven and justified. Christ the final judge is none other than Christ the merciful savior. "To me," writes Luther, "he is a physician, helper and deliverer from death and the devil."

When Jesus says, "Anyone who comes to me I will never drive away" (John 6:37), Luther interprets him to mean,

> Let it be your one concern to come to Me and to have the grace to hold, to believe and to be sure in your heart that I was sent into the world for your sake, that I carried out the will of My Father and was sacrificed for your atonement, righteousness, sanctification and redemption, and bore all punishment for you. If you believe this, do not fear. I do not want to be your judge, executioner or jailer, but your Savior and Mediator, yes, your kind, loving Brother and good Friend. But you must abandon your work-righteousness and remain with Me in firm faith. Divine judgment at the end of history completes divine justification, grounded in Christ's redemptive work, in the middle of history.

Yet it is not clear how the final justification of the ungodly would as such create a world of love, not even if we take it to include what Friedrich Schleiermacher has called the "complete sanctification." No doubt it would ensure that we would meet in the world to come even those whom we have not considered particularly lovable in the present one. But for us to love the unlovable, two things would need to happen.

First, in a carefully specified sense, we ourselves would need to "justify" them, and, given that they may consider us no more lovable than we consider them, they would also need to "justify" us. We would all need to receive this justification from each other. Second, above and beyond giving and receiving justification, we would also need to want to be in communion with one another. To usher in a world of love, the eschatological transition would need to be understood not only as a divine act toward human beings but in the above two senses also as a social event between human beings; more precisely, a divine act toward human beings that is also a social event between them.

Put in the form of a question about the perpetrator and the victim of the first violence in primal history, the challenge that Christian eschatology must meet is this: If Cain and Abel are to meet again in the world to come, what will need to have happened between them for Cain not to keep avoiding Abel's look and for Abel not to want to get out of Cain's way?

Surely the response must go something like this: If the world to come is to be a world of love, then somehow and somewhere in the course of the transition from the present world to that world of perfect love, Cain and Abel must reconcile. The transition must include not only the resurrection of the dead and the last judgment but also the final social reconciliation.

PERSPECTIVE

A Death of a Friend

The recent death of a friend has given me much to think about. His name was Tomislav Simic, but we all called him Toma. He was from Novi Sad, the town in Serbia in which I grew up. When he died, he was fifty-eight.

During his last twenty years or so, Toma spent much of his life confined to psychiatric wards. The dilapidated buildings of these depressing institutions, in a country depleted by reckless wars, were homes to his frail body, confused soul, but alert mind. When living on his own, he frequented soup kitchens because he was too poor to buy his own food. He died in a hospital, where he had been brought because of a high fever and a significant drop in blood pressure. But Toma was a nobody, and so the doctors did not even bother to establish the cause of his death.

Now, as Christians we all know it as an indubitable human truth: *nobody is a nobody!* Yet people are treated as nobodies all the time. Thousands upon thousands die of hunger amidst plenty. Others suffer from easily treatable diseases. Still others are utterly despised because they look or act "weird," and the list goes on. People who are mentally ill are among those most often treated as nobodies. It is not that we relate to them merely as things; for we value many things, whereas we do not value them. We do not even treat them as worthless things; for we simply disregard worthless things, whereas we often feel an aversion, a fundamental hostility toward the mentally ill. When they happen to be very poor, as Toma was, we let them — the ultimate nobodies — die with little regard to their basic human dignity.

When Toma and I became friends, he was somebody! I was sixteen, he was twenty-two, and his body was anything but frail. He was a body builder, one of the best in the country, with aspirations and good prospects of becoming Mr. Universe. But then he embraced the Christian faith and joined the church of which my father was a pastor. He felt that God required of him to abandon his athletic pursuits, which until then were his god. He transposed the dreams of becoming Mr. Universe onto a religious plane: he wanted to be the Apostle Paul of Yugoslavia, and maybe a new Billy Graham to the world. Within a single year, he read the Bible from cover to cover thirteen times. In then-communist Yugoslavia, he spoke about Christ with unusual boldness to anybody and everybody who would listen, whether a crowd gathered in a church or a communist informer poking his nose into others' affairs.

After initial resistance to reading anything other than the Bible — why spend time reading books that are always lesser than the greatest of all books, the very word of God!? — Toma started devouring the great works of Western civilization, those written by the likes of Plato, Thomas Aquinas, Hegel, and Nietzsche. He had a three-year college-level degree in theology, but in philosophy he remained basically self-taught. When I returned to Novi Sad with a master's degree in theology from Fuller Theological Seminary, we had long discussions on Gadamer's *Truth and Method;* he an underemployed Pentecostal evangelist living in a two-room shack with his mother and step-father, had read more of that seminal work than I had, even though I'd studied philosophy and used the book at Fuller as an assigned text!

As soon as he had found his way to faith — as soon as God found a way to him! — a group of teenagers gathered around him in the basement of my dad's church. Some were already church folk, like I was, maybe with an ambivalent relation to faith. Others, many from atheist families, were attracted to the way of Christ through him, directly or indirectly. His successes as an athlete, his devotion to God, his limitless appetite for learning about the Bible and (later) about everything related to it, and his boundless self-confidence pulled many of us into his orbit. It is surprising how many of us from that relatively small group ended up not just in some form of Christian ministry, but with earned doctorates from major academic institutions. Certainly, others have helped and inspired us along the way. But his impetus was crucial — and it remained crucial even when later we felt that he was too sure of himself for his or our good and his orbit was too constricting. His all-encompassing vision, boundless energy, and single-minded dedication passed to us and became *our* vision, energy, and dedication.

From one angle you could say that some of us, his junior friends, succeeded, whereas he failed. We became ministers, professors, administrators of academic institutions, public intellectuals; after a decade or so of activity he, on the other hand, fell into mental illness. In retrospect, the seeds of his future "failure" were discernible in, among other things, the over-the-top character of everything he did. And yet, in a strange way, the seeds of his failure were also the seeds of our success. It is not so much that he failed so that we could succeed. It is rather that through his failure, he succeeded in our successes.

Can an arrow forget the bow that set it flying, asked Søren Kierkegaard rhetorically at one point in *Either/Or*. Many an "arrow" does, even though its very flight is a testimony to the bow's influence. It is especially easy to forget the shaping power of those whom illness takes out of the company of the "sane" and the "respectable." But even when I fail to remember how formative Toma was for me, the trajectory of my life is a silent memorial to him. Even though it was unwitting, maybe his was a truly Christian way of being somebody — being a bow for the flight of others.